Space for Magic

"*Make Space for Magic* is the book you must read if you're blocking abundance and are ready to stop. Patty blends brain science and metaphysical teachings in a way that will make even the most cynical believe magic is available to all of us."

—Barbara Huson, author of *Rewire for Wealth and Overcoming Underearning*

"If there is anything you'd like to change in your life (a relationship, your career, a financial situation, where to live, etc.), then *Make Space for Magic* is THE book to read to make it happen! I laughed, I cried, I learned the three areas in my life that I'm rejecting and how it's keeping me stuck! Patty Lennon skillfully weaves humor, life lessons, and her magical powers to create life changing strategies that I know will work for you."

—Lisa Jones, author of *Art of Living Happy After the Loss of a Loved One*

"*Make Space for Magic* is the book that your heart has been waiting years for you to read. Patty Lennon, with her effortless charm, ancient wisdom, and relentless empathy, takes the reader by the hand and guides them through the wilderness of limited thinking and into a life of abundance. This book will absolutely make you a believer in magic again!"

—John Roedel, author of *Hey God. Hey John.: What Happens When God Writes Back*

"Patty's work occupies an important space in the world of spiritual writing. She has melded wisdom from her traditional Catholic upbringing and subsequent spiritual awakening to forge a practical and magical relationship with the Divine.

Both relatable and comforting, Patty is gifted in her ability to seamlessly weave spiritual lessons into day-to-day experiences such as the struggles of building a business and raising a family and the practicalities of trying to manifest our innermost desires.

Read this book if you've been looking to reconcile your own spiritual beliefs and are seeking a compassionate and pragmatic way to invite Divine magic into your life.

Also read this book if you've ever felt like a spiritual failure. Patty will bring you insight on how you can access your highest levels of manifestation, and, more importantly, she will guide you on the path to Love."

—Anna Tsui, author of *Shadow Magic: Turn Your Fear into Fuel and Create a Prosperous Coaching Business*

"This is a MUST read if you want a life of ease, joy, and magic! The wisdom shared in *Make Space for Magic* will illuminate exactly why things are not flowing for you and the steps to get things moving. Highly recommended!"

—Patricia Lohan, author of *The Happy Home: Your Guide to Creating a Happy, Healthy, Wealthy Life*

"When it comes to spiritual teachers, nobody can make you both laugh AND cry like Patty Lennon! She offers practical tools alongside divine wisdom, blending brain science with metaphysical teachings. Her book, *Make Space for Magic*, is the book we all need to learn how to open ourselves up for abundance, create whatever we desire, and make the most of this precious gift of life!"

—Jennifer Tuma-Young, author of *Balance Is Bunk*

Make
Space
for
Magic

LEARN TO RECEIVE LOVE, ABUNDANCE,
AND SUPPORT FROM THE UNIVERSE

Make
Space
for
Magic

PATTY LENNON

 Published by Mandala Tree Press
www.mandalatreepress.com

Paperback ISBN: 9781954801189
Hardcover ISBN: 9781954801196
eBook ISBN: 9781954801202

SEL016000 SELF-HELP / Personal Growth / Happiness
OCC019000 BODY, MIND & SPIRIT / Inspiration & Personal Growth
SEL032000 SELF-HELP / Spiritual

Cover design by VeryMuchSo Agency
Edited by Justin Greer
Typeset by Kaitlin Barwick

www.pattylennon.com

To Matthew & Katie

My best and favorite teachers

Contents

Contents

Contents

Part III: Receiving 119

Contents

Introduction

When I was seven years old, I knew exactly what I was going to be when I grew up: a missionary. I was going to go out and tell people that God loved them. I would sit with them and love them and show them they were not alone.

I was Catholic, and just to be clear, I didn't want to convince other people to convert to my religion. It never occurred to me that that was part of the job description. It was simply that it broke my heart to think that someone else might be living scared, alone, or in poverty, without knowing that they had this Divine Being who loved them unconditionally.

When I thought about my future, it was impossible to conceive of doing anything else.

And then I became a corporate banker—obviously a career *very* closely related to my childhood dreams.

I didn't set out to become a banker; I fell into it.

By the time I was in college, I had come to realize that my childhood dream of missionary work, albeit altruistic, wasn't realistic. I eventually translated my desire to help others into a desire to become a public defender.

I loved the law and found joy and ease in the college coursework. My senior year, I got a coveted internship with the Broome County Public Defender's Office. At first the work was exciting

1

and fulfilling, but it wasn't long before I recognized the injustice in our justice system.

The public defenders I supported in my internship were nothing less than superheroes in their fight for our clients, but I could see they were set up to fail. As I looked across the landscape of that career, I couldn't step forward.

I had no idea what I was going to do with my life, but I knew it wasn't law.

I left college in 1993 to face a grim job market—which was fine because I'm not sure I would have known what to look for, even if the market was on fire. I applied to a temp agency, and they placed me at a bank.

My uncle owned a finance company and had let me work there during the summer, so I came with some industry background. Without that, I'm not sure I would have even qualified for temp work back then.

The first assignment I received in my new role was to update client mailing addresses in our system. If you've ever filled out a change of address on the back of a billing statement, mailed it in, and wondered how it got updated, I'm going to pull back that curtain for you:

A recent and otherwise unemployable college graduate is sitting at a desk for hours making those keystrokes happen.

Midway through one afternoon, I finished up the stack of address changes I'd been given and asked my manager for more. She said she had left me three piles right by my desk. I told her those were done.

She was in shock and told me that what she gave me would usually take the team a week to process. She told her second-in-command, "Look what Patty just did!"

I'm not going to lie—after feeling lost for so long, the sweet balm of data-processing success felt good.

I arrived at my temp job every day, eager to exceed the very low bar that had been set for me. As a result, my manager noticed and within a few weeks offered me a permanent job.

I knew this wasn't my calling, but it was a paycheck, and it came with the health benefits my parents seemed so fixated on. I took it. It would pay my bills until I figured out what I was going to do with my life.

During the first five years, I walked into that building with the sense that this was a temporary placement. I had absolutely no desire to climb the corporate ladder, but I was a perfectionist heavily addicted to people-pleasing and recognition, so I had a natural propensity to do excellent work and always be on the lookout for how I could help my managers. Without "trying," I was quickly promoted.

Then something shifted. I was recruited onto the team of someone who would become one of my favorite managers. It was a sales position, and I soon found I loved it. The position allowed me to travel and entertain while helping our business clients find financial solutions.

At first the joy of closing a deal carried me along. Eventually the joy of being really good at something propelled me to see banking as a career.

Each year I took on more responsibility and received more accolades, and my original yearning to help people know God's love was sated by the ability to help our clients and our internal team.

When I met my husband at age twenty-nine, I was a vice president of . . . something. Honestly, I can't even remember. But I loved it and then I loved him. We married when I was thirty-one, and we immediately began trying to have children.

Months and months passed, and eventually after a year, my doctor said we needed to consider that one of us was infertile. I remember one night curled up in my bedroom on the floor sobbing. (Side note: I still wonder why I was on the floor. The bed would have been so much more comfortable. Maybe the floor felt a better match for the frustration and desperation I felt.)

It was the first time—but certainly not the last—when my reality so completely opposed what I knew to be true. I *knew* I was meant to have children, and I also knew I wasn't meant to have fertility treatments. Back then I rarely leaned into the intuition that guides my life today, but I did where pregnancy was concerned.

Motherhood would eventually become the thing that awakened me to my own intuition, and this breakdown on the floor was one of the first steps in that direction.

I could feel my children inside my heart, and so I concluded adoption would ultimately be our route. But I was so worn out by all the trying and failing that I needed a break. I needed to regroup and regain my energy for the road ahead.

My husband and I took some time off and headed to Cape Cod to relax. It was early fall, and the Cape was both beautiful and empty—exactly what we needed.

Five weeks later, I was getting ready to check out of my hotel room, having just wrapped up an industry event, when I felt so ill I wasn't sure I was going to be able to handle the drive home. I asked my friend and colleague if I had really drunk enough to make me sick. I only remembered having a few drinks, but our events often ended in the wee hours of the night, and it was possible I had lost track of my consumption.

She laughed at me and said she didn't think so, but maybe I was getting old. Then she looked at me and said, "Something's different." I watched her eyes study my face and then give me a once over.

"Your boobs are bigger!" she exclaimed. "And your face is . . . different. Oh. My. God. Are you pregnant?!"

4

I brushed her off. Of course not. She knew well the struggle we had getting pregnant. It was weird that she even suggested it. She demanded I call Matt, my husband, and have him pick up a pregnancy test so I could take it as soon as I got home.

For months we had bought those tests in bulk. In the first months I took them almost daily when I thought I had missed my period. Just seeing them in the bathroom broke my heart, so I had tossed them weeks before.

I debated on whether I should even call Matt. I didn't want to get his hopes up. I was 99 percent confident I was not pregnant. I mean—you'd know, wouldn't you?

But as I thought back, I realized I was late. I was *very* late.

I called Matt and asked him to get the test. "It's probably nothing, but I feel so nauseous. I just want to rule it out."

That night when I got home, I stepped into Matt's arms and laid my head on his chest—my safe space. The nausea had stopped, and I had already decided it was just the long night that had me feeling ill earlier.

Matt didn't even ask me about taking the test. We had both been through this process so many times, there wasn't room for hope. Once we caught up, I headed up to change.

"Did you put the test in the bathroom?" I asked.

"Sure did. It's under the sink."

I plodded up the stairs, feeling the exhaustion from the long business trip with late nights in my bones.

I pulled off my jacket, stepped out of my suit pants and headed into the bathroom. "Might as well get it over with," I thought.

I peed on the stick like I had done fifty times before, set it down, and proceeded to wash up for the night. By the time my teeth were brushed, I almost forgot the test was there. But it caught my eye as I turned to leave. I picked it up and saw the one thing I had waited so desperately for all those months.

I was pregnant.

As soon as I saw the little "plus" sign, a voice I didn't recognize said, "It's a boy." I thought it was my imagination, so I shook it off and walked into the den where my husband was waiting.

He didn't even look up at me. I'm sure he had forgotten about the test too. You can only take so much pain before your nervous system creates processes to protect you. Both Matt and I had become numb to the answers in a pregnancy test.

"Matt," I said slowly. I wasn't even sure what to say next. How many times had I gotten us both excited by a period that was a few days late? "I think I might be pregnant" had been used so much I couldn't bring myself to even say it.

He was looking at me now. "What?" he said, curious but still not making the connection between me standing there, staring at him, and the pregnancy test.

And that is when the words found me. I didn't think I was pregnant. I *knew* I was pregnant. I had never said those words before.

"We're pregnant."

Motherhood

Our first child, Matthew, was born in 2005. Our miracle.

In 2007, we welcomed our daughter, Katie, into the world.

In the two years after Matthew was born, our world became monumentally busier. Not only were Matt and I juggling children and work, but we were both in school getting master's degrees, Matt in business and me in psychology.

We each held more responsibility in our respective jobs, and I was trying to perform as "star player" for my team with the reduced work hours that let me ensure my children didn't spend all their waking hours in day care.

Matt and I juggled work commitments with getting the kids to day care and scheduling ourselves so one of us was with the kids as much as physically possible.

This meant I was up and out of the house by 7:00 a.m. to get to work by 8:00 so I could leave and pick up the kids by 3:00. To drop the kids off at 9:00, Matt went to work late and therefore was home late.

Matt managed the morning routine of getting the kids dressed, assembling lunches, and getting himself ready, then racing to day care with the hope he'd get to work on time.

I handled the evening routine. I raced to day care in the hopes of getting there before my daughter was put down for a late afternoon nap, which always threw off our schedule.

The guilt of working drove me to "make the most of our time," so as soon as I had the kids with me, I focused all my attention on them. This meant I gave myself zero time to decompress from work or day care pickups.

We came home and immediately jumped into "child-led activities." I threw dinner together, all while keeping eye contact with both kids so they'd know how much they were loved.

Matt got in just in time to have dinner with us most nights. After dinner we jumped into the evening routine, which included baths, stories, and "laying time"—a process that the kids seemed to extend longer and longer every night.

Most nights, once the kids were in bed, I poured myself a glass of wine, needing the support to relax enough to breathe.

I always felt like I was trying to catch up with the mother and employee I knew I should be but kept falling short.

I'd like to say I tried to be the kind of wife I knew I could be, but that would be a lie. I loved my husband, but there was no energy for any aspirational wifeyness. Date nights? What's that?

It wasn't that we didn't love each other. I did and still do love Matt deeply. But once the kids came along, there was just so much to do that finding time for romance felt like a hill I didn't even know how to climb and definitely didn't have the energy for.

I knew I had advantages that most women didn't. I had a fully involved husband/father. The money for good day care. A male boss who understood and valued family balance, appreciated my work, and was happy to let me work reduced hours so my kids weren't in day care ten hours a day.

We had money for a home we owned, two working cars, food, and whatever our kids needed.

We weren't rich, but I knew we were deeply blessed—which is why it was so hard for me to wrap my head around the fact that I could not seem to excel in my work the way I once had. And I never felt that I excelled at motherhood the way I had in other things I had dedicated this much time, research, and effort to.

The Quiet Pulse of "Not Enough"

No matter what I did, there was always a quiet, pulsing voice inside me saying, "Not enough . . . not enough."

From the moment I got up until I went to bed, I was going, going, going—and yet it wasn't enough to be the version of myself I *knew* I could be.

There was, however, one moment each day when I got to slow down and just be. It was my very favorite time of day. I would lay with my son in his bed as he readied himself for sleep, then head into my daughter's room, where I would hold her in the darkness, rocking back and forth.

My son had always been a high-energy dude from the moment he came into the world. He needed a lot of interaction to be satisfied to slip off into dreamland. But my daughter was the complete opposite. Put her down and she'd go to sleep—not a peep out of her.

That rocking time was for me.

I'd rest her big baby chubbiness in my arms, grounded by the sheer volume of her, and rock. Sometimes she'd look at me. Other times she'd stare off just over my shoulder but always so still—so quiet—so peaceful, as if to say, "It's okay, Mom. You let me know when you're ready to let go."

It was as close to meditation as I could get back then. So it was really startling one night as we sat there and rocked and her body jerked. Just as quickly, she settled down—until a few moments later, when the same thing happened again.

I leaned closer in the darkness to see if her little baby face was scrunched up in pain or distress, but . . . nope. Just her peaceful little self staring back at me. That's when I noticed the drops of water on her cheek. Where did they come from?

I looked up, expecting to see a leak in the ceiling, but even in the darkness, I could see it was dry. And that was when I realized that water was mine. Those drops were my tears.

I sat, dumbfounded, trying to find the reason why there were tears pouring down my cheeks and how I didn't know there were tears pouring down my cheeks. As the seconds ticked by, the reality of where I was, who I was, and how I felt closed in.

Deep down inside me, I was sad, deeply sad. But more frightening was the fact that until that moment, I had no idea. Because wrapped tightly around all that sadness was numbness. Somehow, I had turned the dial on my own inner truth to "mute."

As I breathed into this sadness, the layers of everything I felt started to float to the top—the pressure of trying to excel at a job I was doing in half the time it needed, the loss of my personal freedom, and worst of all, the overwhelming pressure of being a mom to two little ones.

I was instantly disgusted with myself. I knew how much I had to be grateful for. I had so much—the greatest of which was two healthy kids. I was holding this precious human and feeling BAD.

You Deserve Better

As I looked at my daughter I thought, "You deserve so much better than me."

Just as that thought crystallized, an energy swooshed into the room, and a voice I have learned to trust as my grandmother said, quite frankly, "Then become the mother she deserves to have."

At that moment, I thought what my grandmother was trying to tell me was to become a mother who appreciates what she has, and in a way, that *is* what she was telling me. But what she really wanted me to know, what she was insisting on, was that I become a mother who is happy.

A mother who could show my children what a life of possibility and joy and hope and love looks like. A life that felt free, not burdened. And in order to become that kind of mother, I had to have a life of possibility and joy and hope and love.

I needed to become free.

If you had told *that* version of myself that that was what I needed, I would have told you it would require a big heaping dose of magic to make it happen. And although back then I believed in magic, I always felt it was for other people, not for me.

I'm not sure why I thought magic existed for someone else but not me. Maybe because I felt I had so many blessings, I thought I shouldn't need magic to thrive. Or maybe it was that bringing magic into life required some sort of skill set I didn't have. Either way, it would have been really hard for me to wrap my head around the fact that magic was available to me in every moment.

What would have been even more unbelievable to me was that twelve years later, I would be sitting here, writing you this love letter of a book, trying to explain exactly how I called that magic in and exactly how I turned a life of overwhelm and obligations to a life filled with possibility, freedom, and joy.

I would never have been able to envision a future where I spend my days leading people to the same opportunities. That version of me would have a hard time believing I would go on to create The Receiving School®, where people would join me from around the world learning how to allow in the money, love, support, and intuitive guidance the Divine offers us each day.

I would have struggled to believe any of that. But I think if someone I trusted had whispered to my 2008 self the words I am about to whisper to you, my soul would have heard and believed this much to be true:

You can create space for magic.

Part I

Awareness

Chapter 1

What Does "Space for Magic" Mean?

You may be wondering what "magic" even means. Am I talking about casting spells and using magic wands? No, not really (although if that feels fun for you, go for it).

According to Merriam-Webster, magic is the power of apparently influencing the course of events by using mysterious or supernatural forces.[1]

And therein lies the reason most people do not experience the magic they have available to them.

We are taught to believe that magic happens when someone has the "power to influence," yet it's often when we feel the most powerless that the magic arrives—or, at the very least, it's when we feel the least capable of influencing events or people that the magic is most useful.

So I'd like to propose a different definition of magic for the purpose of our time together. Let's think of magic as the experience of transcending our own personal (perceived) human limitation.

---

1. See the entry for "magic" at https://www.merriam-webster.com/dictionary /magic.

Taken one step further, magic is what happens when we choose to allow in experiences, results, material wealth, and even happiness that we don't believe the human part of us has the power to create.

Which begs the question—if the human part of us is not creating magic, who or what is?

Where does magic come from?

I'm going to call that force the Divine. Sometimes I will call it God or the Universe. You replace my words with whatever works for you. You might call it "Source," "Allah," or something else, but at its essence, it is the truth of what we are made of and from. Its essence is love.

Magic is the force that creates a bridge between where you currently are and what you desire. It makes life easier and more fulfilling because when magic is at play, you no longer need to rely on your effort alone. You can trust that even if you rest, things are still happening.

You can start to see this force is available to ALL people equally, so you will no longer feel the burden of having to be the sole provider of care, love, and help to so many.

You can start to give more space to BIG DREAMS because now you realize you don't need to wait for everyone else to be raised, fed, and taken care of before you can look to manifest something meaningful to your soul.

You'll learn that you don't have to MAKE more money to have more money.

You can have the life you've dreamed of—but first, you'll need to *make space for magic*.

It is likely that over the years, you have eliminated space for magic in your life. You didn't mean to. It happened in the most innocent of ways at first. But you've learned to cling to what you can do and control rather than to surrender to a power beyond your own human efforts.

I know. I did the same thing. I built the life. I cultivated a career. I found my partner. I had my kids. I took care of my parents. I contributed to my community. I was a good person who did my best.

When I was young, my ability to do it "by myself" was what gave me a sense of control and safety. And the more effective I became at solving my own problems and helping the people around me, the more my community (parents, teachers, peers) made me feel like I was on the right track.

I learned early on that needing help made me a burden and extreme independence made me acceptable and lovable. It took me decades to understand that extreme independence is actually a trauma response, but I'll talk about that later.

The point is that my aversion to needing help was how I shut out space for magic, and I'm guessing it was the same for you. In contrast, learning to ask for and receive help is how we create space for magic.

I have spent the last twelve years unwinding my toxic relationship with extreme independence, learning to trust the support available to me at all times, and realizing that my needs add to my lovability, not detract from it.

I have learned to create space for magic, and I want to help you do that as well.

The Real Gift

Magic has brought all sorts of cool and amazing things into my life—but that isn't what I want you to focus on or why I want you to keep reading. Yes, making space for magic has helped me pay off six figures of debt, come into a peaceful and easy relationship with my two teen kids, take my marriage to a depth I dreamed of as a little girl, obtain "best seller" credentials, and grow a business I love. But that isn't the best part. Creating space for magic has shown me what it feels like to experience true safety—safety that isn't controlled by external circumstances like money, career, or other people's reactions to me.

I feel safe even when challenges arise, life gets chaotic, or something doesn't work out the way I thought it would. In fact, challenges and unexpected chaos no longer signal that something is wrong but now mean something even better is on its way. How exciting!

Creating space for magic has taught me how to feel alive— 100 percent alive and on purpose in a way I hadn't experienced since childhood.

Making space for magic has taught me to love and heal and hope.

Making space for magic allows me to wake up every morning and know, no matter what happens, that there is a force in my life that is bigger than my own human limitations. It reassures me that I can use and trust that force at every minute of every day, and that is what makes me feel safe, even when I didn't know I was scared.

That's what I want for you.

I see you. I know how hard you try to get it all right. I know how often you feel you've let other people or yourself down. I know how unfair your burden feels—and how you still silently blame yourself for not being strong enough to rise above it.

But please listen to me. If you don't turn another page in this book, please know this: the Divine sees you and loves you just as you are. You have always done your very best with what you have, and the Divine wants to reward you. Your burden is not your fault—it's simply a sign that you need help. And it doesn't matter if you can't imagine where that help will come from. In fact, it's even better if you don't, because that will make the help feel that much more magical.

You are loved. You are precious. You are worthy. You are more than enough.

I also know that you are tired and overwhelmed. You don't have the energy to learn how to "create space for magic." In fact, even now, you may be wondering if you should pour yourself a(nother) glass of wine, shut this book, and watch Netflix. That is about as close to magic as you can really believe in.

I get it. Close the book if you need to. Drink the wine. Numb out on Netflix if you must. But just know this: it doesn't have to be hard.

Remember Who You Are

You don't have to *learn* how to create space for magic; you just have to *remember* how to do it.

When you came to this planet, you had 100 percent faith in the magic available to you and knew exactly how to use it. You still have a built-in system to guide you on your path, and it is calibrated to attract and receive the perfect amount of magic to make your life run for your soul's highest good.

But over time, life experiences and other people taught you something different.

As a baby, you looked around your world and without hesitation demanded everything you needed, expecting it to show up. The thought that you shouldn't ask or that you wouldn't receive that help just didn't exist.

Then someone taught you something different. Most likely, that someone loved you very much and never intended to teach you limitations, but they did. How could they not, when they themselves had been taught limitations?

Even in the most loving environments, here's a pretty typical way this goes down.

You are a baby. You have loving parents who care for you deeply. You are fed, clothed, and cuddled. And one day you reward those parents for their efforts with a smile. You weren't trying to "reward" them—you simply felt things that made your lips turn up at the corners, and boom—fireworks.

Those parents are thrilled. You see it in their faces—so much happiness—and somehow you know you did that. Little old vulnerable you, who has very little control in your life, gave something to the people you loved, and it mattered.

Then it happens again. A burbling sensation starts in your little belly, and before you know it, those lips are pointing up again! And your people are so happy! And you did it!

You love these people, and you want to keep making them feel this way. So you learn how to make those lips move when you want them to because, oh man, it feels so good to watch their faces light up.

And in that innocent beautiful moment, a thought process begins to form that you have the power to affect how other people feel.

A few days or months later, you are sick. You don't feel good, and you are crying because that is the only way to let your people know you need help. They rush to you, but they can't seem to fix what hurts—and what's worse, you can see that your crying is making them feel bad.

You start to understand that not all your needs are good. Some of your needs upset the people you love.

At first, you can't control your needs or crying because, well, you are a baby. But as you get older, learning how to need less and give more becomes important to you.

And as you learn these skills of needing less and giving more, you receive praise, acceptance, and approval, which your brain equates to safety.

Fast forward twenty, thirty, or forty years later, and BAM—you have defined your success by the ability to need less and give more, and your ability to allow in help has disappeared because being needy is not safe.

You have learned what success looks like "out there," and you keep striving for it. In the process you've blocked the space for magic. You "get it done," but what happens when there isn't enough of you to get any more done?

What happens when your body starts shutting down because of exhaustion?

Or you start shutting down within your relationships because you can barely keep all the plates spinning, and focusing on your people keeps you from focusing on those plates. What do you do then?

When the Plates Begin to Fall

Because here's the thing—all those plates you keep spinning? One of them is about to fall, and from my experience, once one starts to fall, a few more will follow along. At first it will feel like you are doing something wrong in letting those plates fall.

You'll search for time-management courses or self-improvement courses that promise to help you get back to spinning all those plates. But eventually, if you're lucky, one day you'll end up exactly where I did. You'll realize that spinning all those plates is making you numb with exhaustion, and you'll want something different.

In fact, you might even notice that having a few of those plates in tiny pieces on the floor is a relief! "Ah well, I screwed that up, but at least I don't have to do it anymore." And that relief is just the first taste of what else is possible.

That relief will guide you straight out of your overworking, overtrying half-life and right onto a path filled with so much more. When you want that relief more than the accolades of spinning all those plates, then you are ready to create space for magic!

Chapter 2
Why It Matters

"We regret to inform you . . ."

On March 5, 2019, two police officers showed up at my door.

"Are you Patricia Lennon?" they asked.

"I am . . ."

"Ma'am, we regret to inform you that your father passed away."

Fifteen minutes later, I was standing in my dad's bedroom. I asked the police officer who had stayed with his body to leave me alone with him. I told my husband the same thing.

I sat down on the bed next to where my dad lay. I looked around, searching for signs of what his last moments were like. Were there signs of struggle? I didn't see any.

He was simply lying there, peaceful.

The Space for Goodbye

I took his hand in mine. I ran my hand over each knuckle, feeling the smoothness of his skin. I rubbed the ruby stone in his college ring. My dad wasn't a material person, but he loved that ring. He never took it off.

Time slowed as I held his hand in mine. I knew he wasn't there in that body anymore, but I wanted to drink in these last moments with him.

As I sat there with him, I thanked him for being my dad. I felt the life we had together expand and contract in the room. Pieces of my childhood floated into me, and I blew them back out to him—little love notes in the ethers.

I told him how much I missed him already, even though I knew I had yet to feel the waves of grief that would come.

I wouldn't have been able to have those moments with my dad a few years earlier, before I had learned to slow down and be part of each moment. Most of my life, I rushed from one obligation to the next, focusing more on what others might think of me than anything else.

For so many years, my mind had run through a consistent loop of what others might need from me and what I needed to do in order to be a good wife/mother/daughter/friend/employee.

Even as I sat there, saying goodbye to my father, that old pattern in my mind tried to take over. "You know there is an officer waiting out there—you are probably holding him up!" and "You never offered him a drink—what if he's thirsty?"

I could hear that part of me serve up its list of worries, but it held no power.

I had learned how to live inside moments—especially the important ones. I had learned how to drop into my soul and feel where it was calling me. My soul knew what I really needed, even while my mind tried to convince me that what others might need should come first.

My mind wanted to take care of the police officer. My soul said, "Stay here. Be here."

When that small voice couldn't distract me with the needs of the police officer, it tried to push different buttons.

"You are selfish sitting here—holding on to this moment with your dad when your sister and brother don't even know he's gone yet. Get off this bed and call them. This isn't about you!"

But even that held no power over me. This, me + my dad, had to come first, and my soul understood that. In the days and weeks that followed, I would be there to help everyone else say goodbye, but first I had to let myself say goodbye.

Learning how to fulfill my own needs before I reached out to care for others was a long process but an important one. It gave me these precious minutes alone with my dad.

In that bedroom, the energy pulsed out and in, first as a bubble wrapped closely around my dad and me, but as the moments passed and I let myself breathe, I felt the love. First it was the love I had for my dad flowing out, then eventually I could feel it return—his love for me.

Soon the room was filled with love. I could feel the others—my mother, my ancestors, my Spirit Guides—standing watch, waiting to catch me if and when I needed it. That ordinary bedroom became a sacred space.

And even as the tears poured down my face, I felt safe. I felt deep sadness. I felt the loss of my father in every cell of my body, but I did not feel alone. I felt love.

When people come to this work of receiving, of creating space for the magic and love of the Universe to fill their lives, they often want the tangible benefits—more money, partnership, support. All those things are good and beautiful, but it's these quiet moments that are the real gold.

The greatest treasure is to be able to drop into the sacred space our life creates and hold it. To experience the waves of love and support we have from the Divine and our ancestors in our darkest moments. This is what changes the quality of our lives.

Learning to Slow Down

I could tell you a thousand stories right now that would show you why it's important to create space for magic, what it means to create space for magic, what that magic can give you.

I could tell you about the money that has flowed into my life and the lives of my clients. I could tell you how challenges that seemed impossible to overcome were resolved with ease. I could tell you about the relationships that grew, the partnerships created.

The miracles are truly endless, but that moment with my dad is the one I wanted you to hear first. Because to me, this is the real gift of creating space for magic: to walk through the world, being present in the moments that count—because you know that no matter what happens, you are safe and loved.

Safety for each of us means one thing: knowing that we will be okay. But most of us create dysfunctional ways to feel safe. We try to control as much as possible so we can create the outcome we want, which often involves taking on the burdens of others. Or we take certain action to make sure we keep the approval of others.

The problem with these strategies is that no matter how hard we try, we can't control outcomes all the time, and we can't always make people approve of us, so we end up in a constant cycle of chasing safety rather than experiencing it. Rather than experiencing life, we are constantly scanning for what actions we might need to take to feel safe.

When we learn to release these dysfunction patterns in favor of trusting the Divine and receiving the gifts the Divine sends us—including protection—we can drop into each moment.

When I look back over my life and see what it used to be like and what it's like now, what really stands out is how much more *in my life* I am. There is depth and richness in each moment, and I missed so much of that before I learned to slow down and create this space.

Trust me—I know it can be scary to let go of that constant striving and reaching for the "better" version of you. The persistent watchfulness that you may need to do something because you can't trust your partner, children, or loved ones to do it properly. Over our lifetime we come to believe that what makes us worthy is what others think of us, when the truth is that we are worthy just as we are.

Creating space for magic happens when you start to believe in your own worthiness. Then you can trust that whatever you need in any moment is available to you, and your only "work" is to receive it.

Hitting Your "Manifestation" Ceiling

Are you familiar with the Law of Attraction? It's the idea that our reality is a reflection of our energetic vibration. In order to attract a better reality, we need to improve our vibration. If you have read books or taken course on how to use the Law of Attraction, you have probably learned that in order to manifest a desire, you must

- visualize your desire.
- act as if you already have it.
- create a vision board.
- affirm.
- vibrate higher.

Maybe you've done those things. In the beginning, it was fun because little bursts of magic happened. A surprising amount of money showed up. A parking spot appeared when you most needed it. Maybe even a certifiable miracle happened.

It worked. Your Law of Attraction or manifestation "work" created a result. So you did more and more of it—but somewhere along the way, the effectiveness of what you were doing dropped off. You got a little money but not enough to really shift your life. A problem you had at work was resolved, but another one popped up in its place. Your kids spontaneously told you that you were a great mom and you felt great, but by the next day you had sixteen reasons to question your ability to hold your house together.

There is a reason why the Law of Attraction works and why it stops working. I'm going to explain what needs to shift to permanently open up space for your deepest desires to manifest fully. The good news is that you don't need to visualize, affirm, vision board, or any of those other things that probably feel like "work" at this point.

The Universe Does Not Require a Vision Board

Think about it. The Universe, the Divine, Source—whatever word you use to refer to the power behind all that manifesting—is all-knowing. Does it make sense that the Divine needs you to cut out pictures and paste them to a piece of poster board to see in your heart that you'd really like to have a vacation with your family where you'll be happy and warm and splashing in crystal-clear blue waters?

Or that She'd make you spell it out in present tense exactly as you want it before She'd deem you worthy of being able to pay your bills with ease and spend time, relaxed and happy, with the people you love?

Of course not! Deep down inside, you must know it has to be easier than this.

It is!

The moment our soul gives birth to a desire, the Universe starts to meet that desire. We are by nature the Divine, and so we already possess the internal power required to bring any desire to life.

If that's true, you're probably wondering, why don't we all have our ideal lives? The answer is that although our desires are in the process of being met every minute of every day, we hold resistance to *allowing* those desires to be met.

It is that *resistance* that keeps our desires at arm's length. It is the reason you can feel that you are meant to have or be or do something but can't quite reach it. The Divine in you knows it is there, but the HUMAN part of you resists.

This resistance is what blocks "magic."

Most manifestation teachers focus on how to ask for what you desire, but what they rarely talk about is how to receive what you most want and need. What you are able to manifest is limited by what you are able to receive.

Releasing resistance is what opens you up to receiving and creates space for magic. That is what I've learned to do over these last twelve years. I call it The Receiving Method™, and it's what I'll teach you throughout this book.

Escaping "Big Success, Big Stress" Syndrome

When Terez joined The Receiving School® and started to apply The Receiving Method™, she knew "receiving" was a block for her. She was great at bringing big dreams to life—she started and grew three completely different businesses. In each case, she reached a point where she had surpassed the success most entrepreneurs experience.

But in each case, when it started to seem that it was "too good to be true," something would tip. Expenses would start to exceed profits, and Terez would end up in a cycle of overworking and stress, eventually exiting each business because the effort to keep it afloat wasn't worth it.

She started to understand that although joy had led her into each business, her fear of the "next level" would eventually create resistance. That resistance would shift her out of the flow she experienced at the start of each business and into the overworking and stress she found at the end.

When she joined The Receiving School®, she had just closed her restaurant of thirty years. The pandemic had changed the world, and she wasn't sure what to do next. She and her husband still had debt that needed to be paid off, but the thought of facing that mountain felt too big.

As we worked together, Terez learned how to tap back into the flow of her own intuition and find the wave of "magic" that had carried her to success in the past. What she realized was that the wave was urging her to slow down and rest, so she did.

After eight weeks of mostly resting, that magic started to show itself in wonderful ways. An unexpected inheritance arrived that allowed her to pay off her debts, and she connected to a deep longing to paint that she thought she'd lost.

She had enjoyed a modest income from her paintings in the past, and now that she was tapped back in, she knew that her art was calling her forward.

She also started to see that each time her business had turned from joy to stress, there had been warning signs she ignored. Right before her business tipped in the "wrong" direction, she had started to feel weary. The Universe had asked her to slow down, pace herself, rest. But she ignored them, and that blocked the flow that had created her original success.

Releasing or letting go of her need to "go, go, go" opened up money flow and her creative spirit again.

As Terez started to paint more, she told me she felt more like herself than she had in years. There was still a bit of an urge to push her success, but now that she understood her big work was to relax and do what felt inspired, she was committed to sticking with the process—the process you'll learn in this book.

The Pulse of Something Better

Have you sensed that you are meant to have more, do more, be more? Can you feel the pulse of something bigger or better waiting for you—if you could just catch up with it? Or get out of the way of it?

If you're like me, you've probably already started flipping through the book, trying to find the part where I tell you step by step what to do to release your own resistance and get the money, creativity, or support flowing in your life.

I get it—but please stick with me and don't skip ahead! The stories and the explanations I share along the way are as much a part of the process of releasing as the actual steps of The Receiving Method™.

That being said, there is something in Terez's story that can show you what to do right now to release some of your resistance: relax. Sit back, pour yourself a cup of coffee (or tea), and enjoy this journey.

If you do that, you'll already be shifting the energy in your life, and without doing anything more, you'll start to receive—just watch!

Chapter 3

Blocking Magic

Six years ago, I was driving home from my favorite yoga class, feeling like I was on top of the world. We had just moved into a new home—our forever home. My speaking schedule was booked out a full year, and my business was thriving. Our kids were in a new school they loved, and everything felt right with the world.

I pulled into our driveway, ready to hop out, shower, and get my day started. But the Universe had other plans for me. The minute I moved my left foot out the door, a searing pain surged up my back. I slowly pulled my leg back in, inch by agonizing inch.

I sat there for hours and was eventually able to crawl inside. When my husband came home, he helped me into bed. I stayed there all weekend until my doctor could see me on Monday.

He thought I had a herniated disc and sent me to a specialist.

After a week filled with doctor's appointments and x-rays, I learned the base of my spine was fractured—and it had been since I was seven.

You may be wondering (as I did) how someone can walk around for thirty-five years with a broken back and have no idea they were injured.

The doctors explained the technical reason is that the injury, which occurs in a small percentage of young girls between the age of seven and eight, is like a ticking time bomb. If you don't know that it's there you can live with it for years, but eventually the crack will make itself known.

What I've since come to realize is that we all walk around this way on some level, with cracks in the foundation of who we are—wounds waiting like little ticking time bombs to reveal themselves when we are ready to heal.

Healing Cracks the Foundation

I engaged Western medicine's approach to healing my back—which included varying forms of physical therapy—but I was more intrigued to understand what the injury meant on a spiritual level.

For a few years I had been playing with various types of self-healing through meditation and "listening" to my body, the theory being that all physical issues are symptoms of deeper emotional issues, and when the emotions are processed, the symptoms are released.

Each day I'd sit in meditation and ask my spine to tell me what it needed me to know. This process had helped me clear colds, sinus infections, and varying minor issues in the past. I was curious to see what would show up here. But each day my questioning was only met with a brick wall of silence.

Finally, one day I asked a different question: "What happened when I was seven to cause this fracture?"

Immediately I heard a voice answer, "You stopped flying."

Suddenly, I saw myself as a young girl of five, maybe six, standing at the edge of our staircase.

I look down and see little toes—my toes—wrapped around the edge of the top step.

I'm not nervous or scared. I'm poised, ready for flight.

It is so clear to me—as clear now as it was completely unclear moments ago.

This is my house. The house I grew up in. The dark wood railing, the white spindles, the wallpaper from my childhood.

The house is dark and quiet. It's the middle of the night. The moonlight pours in the window behind me. I'm standing on the landing and can almost feel the night air calling to me.

I know this place. I've been here before.

I can fly, and I'm getting ready to take off.

I do this at night because grown-ups can't see. It's not that they wouldn't understand or that they'd try to stop me; it's more that when I fly, I'm a part of another life altogether, one that does not involve them.

I already know what comes next. I want to brace for it, but I know I don't have to. So I sit calmly and wait. I wait for this little girl version of me to be ready.

She is.

I bend my legs, push off, and—FLY!

I am literally freaking flying!

Down the stairs, out the front door, I swoop and soar.

Is this real?

I shared this story with a group of clients recently and their immediate question was, "Was that real? Could you really fly?"

The answer is I don't know. It certainly feels as real as any other memory I have ever experienced. I told them it wasn't that important whether it was real or not.

What matters is that as a small child, I felt like I could fly, and one day I just stopped.

Everyone is born knowing how to fly. We are born believing in limitless possibilities—and then we are taught fear. We are taught that flying is dangerous. We are taught that the ground is safe. What we can touch and feel is what we should believe in.

These messages create real-life fractures inside us because they counter what we know is fundamentally true. They "break" our understanding of how powerful we are and how fully the Universe supports our path.

We are "broken" by the grown-ups in our lives who have nothing but our best interests at heart. They just want us to be safe, and they are simply passing on their own inherited and created fears.

Our grown-ups were taught that the world is not safe, that if something is going to happen, they have to make it happen. They were taught there is no magic. There is no flying. And believing in it is unsafe.

We learn to shrink our hopes and dreams to fit within what we can control and create with our own human limitations. We keep the dreams we pursue small so that we can guarantee success for ourselves. We limit ourselves by what we know we can accomplish because we fear the judgment and rejection of others.

And all these fears stem from a belief that we are "not enough."

Learning Not-Enough-ness

We are taught our "not-enough-ness" in a thousand different ways, spoken and unspoken.

This "not-enough-ness" makes the world feel unsafe, and we are taught to focus on filling up the not-enough-ness—rather than reaching for the "everything" we were promised by our Divine parent at birth.

The slow steady beat of "not-enough-ness" motivated everything I did as a child. In fact, until that memory of flying spontaneously dropped in, I could not recall a single time as a child I had felt that free and limitless . . . and yet I must have.

Looking back on it all, I can see it was simply that I felt how much "not-enough-ness" existed in my parents, and I wanted to fill it all up for them. Because I never could, I was always operating at "not enough."

I was the perfect daughter—as much as I had the power to be.

I was great at school, helped around the house. I didn't talk back and tried to ask for as little as possible. Without knowing it, I understood that money had a lot to do with enough-ness, and therefore its absence created not-enough-ness.

Now having worked with hundreds of women one on one and thousands more from stages, I can tell you that the relationship between money and the space for magic is a strong one. It doesn't matter if there was a lot of money or a little money in your home growing up. It was the relationship to what money meant in your childhood home that often removed any space for magic.

The Whisper of "Never Enough"

In school, I remember working on the short story "The Rocking Horse Winner" by D. H. Lawrence. The story is about a family who lived "beyond their means," and the feeling that there was never enough was felt to the point that the children said they heard the house whisper, "There must be more money."

The teacher asked us questions about the story, and I remember her being so thrilled with my answer. I had connected the dots—the house wasn't actually whispering, but the children could feel their parents' feelings and interpreted them as the house whispering.

That memory stands out to me because I was very young and none of the other students seemed to see what I saw in that story, so I felt special. And the teacher was clearly beside herself with joy that I had this insight, so I felt REALLY special.

At the time I would have told you that story had nothing to do with my family. My parents never lived beyond their means; in fact, as Depression-era kids, they were just the opposite—always conservative in their spending. But that whisper . . . my little self recognized that whisper.

I think ours sounded more like, "There isn't enough money," and my little self translated the feeling to mean, "There isn't enough me."

I have seen this same whisper play out in households of every economic persuasion.

A few years ago, as part of an exercise to earn a Girl Scout badge, I asked each child in my daughter's Girl Scout troop who they wanted to *become* when they were older. (I very specifically did not ask them what they would *do* when they got older.)

Even so, one girl—whose family seemed to make significant income—said, "I want to become someone who makes six million dollars." When I asked her why, she told me that "six million dollars is how much money we need before my mom can slow down. It is definitely not just a million."

I know her parents. They are good people. They love their kids and work hard to give them every opportunity in the world. Their daughter has a generous heart. She is always the first to volunteer her allowance to help others. They have a beautiful home and cars and go on wonderful vacations.

But even in the midst of so much abundance, somehow she heard the whisper "not enough."

Although money is often the "thing" we attach the "not enough" to, it shows up in other ways. It can be in relationships—especially romantic relationships—or other forms of material wealth like homes, experiences, or professional success.

Underneath this drive to get more money, a romantic partner, a different home, or a particular type of job or career is really the drive to feel safe. It's a belief that something outside ourselves has the power to make us safe, when in reality, we are safe right now. And when we start to believe that, we create space for magic.

This feeling of "not enough" is what keeps most people from accessing the magic that is readily available to them. We believe some people are more "lucky," have more "advantages," are "set up for success"—when really what we are saying is that some people seem to be more "enough" than us.

For me, my "enough-ness" was tied directly to my ability to make the people around me happier, especially my mother and father, so when something I did—directly or indirectly—seemed to cause them any type of pain or burden, I felt like I had failed.

My client Wendi had a similar experience growing up. She learned from a young age that she was "good" when she supported other people and "bad" when she needed anything.

She was never told this directly. She had good, loving parents, just like I did. But like me, she felt the weight of the burdens her parents carried and wanted nothing more than to lessen those burdens and avoid adding to them.

When I met Wendi, she was an overworked, overstressed corporate achiever. Pre-marriage and pre-kids, achieving at a level that felt "safe" to her was easy. She was a woman who made things happen.

But as she got older and the responsibilities that came with aging parents, marriage, and motherhood added to her load, she felt she was constantly scrambling to succeed the way she wanted to—especially in motherhood.

When she realized she needed to leave the corporate world and venture out on her own in order to find the balance she so desperately wanted, she hit internal block after internal block.

Even though she was looking to make a change for the sake of the people she loved, the choices she needed to make to create that change also felt selfish. Eventually she learned to allow in help from the Divine and the outcome was positively magical.

She launched a business and created $250k in revenue in the first few months. And she found a way to spend the time she wanted with her daughter and be present in her life the way she desired.

But the road there definitely had bumps. The biggest lesson she had to "unlearn" was that she didn't always have to be "okay." She didn't always have to be the cheerleader, and it was okay to need help.

She accepted that she was drained from years of juggling a demanding career and motherhood. She agreed to schedule time off, even though her mind told her to work on her business nonstop until it was successful.

She allowed her daughter to make choices on how she spent her time, rather than trying to micromanage her through a pandemic.

She initially had no "proof" that these changes would create the positive outcome she desired, but she agreed to take the leap of faith and trust her body's need for rest and her daughter's ability to choose for herself.

By opening up to the possibility that her desires could be met even when she rested and released control, she released the blocks to magic she'd been holding.

Chapter 4

Manifestation Myth

It's likely this isn't the first book you've read about spiritual or manifestation principles. You probably fall in one of two groups. Maybe you've been studying spiritual principles for years and have found great resonance with that work. If that's the case, this book is one more in your journey of understanding what is possible when working with the metaphysical realm. If the vision boards and visualization techniques I mentioned earlier bring you joy, continue to do them because the joy is what makes them effective!

The other (more likely) possibility is that you've read a book or two on the Law of Attraction and manifestation, had some small success, but still consider people who play in the "woo" world to be different from you and creating one more vision board just feels exhausting.

In either case, what you've learned hasn't created the miracles you know are possible. You know there's a missing piece or a missing step, but you just aren't sure what that is. Well, the good news is I know what the missing step is, and I'm going to share it with you in this book.

Before I get there, I want to explain to you why what you've done in the past involving "manifestation work" hasn't worked the way you would like it to work. This is what I call "The Manifestation Myth."

When I first encountered the Law of Attraction as a formal "teaching," I was in my late twenties. Once I understood what the Law of Attraction was and how it worked, I realized I had experienced the Law of Attraction at work my whole life. What changed for me when I started to study it was that I was more easily able to consciously employ my thoughts to create shifts and changes.

Before that, I was as far from "woo" as a person could get.

Waking Up

Having been raised in a very traditional Irish-Catholic home, I had never strayed from the Holy Trinity—the Father (masculine "God"), the Son (Jesus), and the Holy Spirit. The way I grew up, if you were looking for a miracle, the Trinity was where you found it. Or, in a pinch, Mother Mary (Jesus's mom). If something was beyond your human ability to bring to life, you prayed. Period. End of discussion.

Then, right around the age of twenty-five, I had a dream that woke me up to a possibility outside my traditional Christian paradigm. The dream was like nothing I had ever experienced. I was in a box—a coffin—but I wasn't scared. I was at peace. The coffin was simple, made of raw wood. The coffin was sitting on top of a table, and I knew I was in a saloon. I could see everyone around me, and my clothes looked like something out of *Little House on the Prairie*. I knew I was at my own wake. These people were here to say goodbye to me.

As soon as I woke up from that dream, I knew this had been a past life. The Catholic Church teaches that we have only this life, so reincarnation was not something I had considered, but waking up from that dream unlocked some deep truth inside me. There were more lives than this one. I could now feel the truth in that. There was a bigger picture to this world than I understood.

I didn't do much with that information for a year, just let it roll around in my mind. But eventually I got curious and started purchasing books written by people who had connections to past lives. That led me to books about near-death experiences, and over the next couple of years I found myself diving deeper and deeper down the rabbit hole of spiritual and metaphysical learning.

So when I found Law of Attraction work, which showed me I had the power to create my reality simply by shifting my vibration, I was hooked. The Law of Attraction filled in a missing piece in what I had been taught about God and miracles. I had always suspected there was more to the story than what the nuns had told us in school about praying hard.

I mean, I knew friends who didn't pray AT ALL and seemed to get everything their heart desired. Life just came easier for them. Surely, if praying was the key to it all, I, a very good Irish-Catholic girl, would have more to show for my efforts.

In fact, as my career had developed in the banking world, I could see that my attitude and confidence were inextricably linked to my success and the success of people around me.

The Law of Attraction made sense of all these disparate parts of my experiences. The Law of Attraction states that the way we think and how we "vibrate" determines what we magnetize to our life. Good thoughts = good things. And of course, the shadow side of this is that if you think negative thoughts, you will call in negative experiences.

Toxic Positivity

This last part—that feeling negative feelings attracts terrible things to us—is the shadow teaching of this work and where I part ways with what has been traditionally been taught in the Law of Attraction world.

This idea that we can't have negative feelings if we are going to have a good life—or at minimum, that we need to work hard to clear that negativity constantly—contributes in a big way to what I call the Manifestation Myth. Now that I teach others how to create a life of possibility and work with the "unseen" forces that are here to help us, I find this "negative thoughts = negative experiences" paradigm to be one of the most harmful teachings across all spiritual traditions—especially Law of Attraction work.

I say this because of the destructive psychological and emotional effects I've witnessed in my clients—and experienced myself—when you try to suppress natural negative emotions.

Take Elizabeth, one of my clients. When she joined The Receiving School®, we were six months into the pandemic. She had lost her job in finance just before COVID moved everyone into sudden isolation. She was looking for a job, but finding one in the midst of layoffs and with NYC in total shutdown felt impossible. She continued to network and do outreach, but it felt *hard*. On top of that, Elizabeth lived alone. She had always enjoyed being the fun aunt that doted on her nieces and nephews and enjoyed the freedom to travel regularly. But with COVID, she couldn't see her family, and travel was out of the question.

On one of our calls, she said, "I'm trying to stay positive. Can you give me any advice on how to do that?"

At that point, I lovingly pointed out that she was in a really challenging situation and that it was okay to feel bad about that.

"But the Law of Attraction says that if we think negative thoughts, we attract more of that into our lives! I don't want any more negative stuff showing up!"

Man, if I had a nickel for every time I've heard that fear uttered! It drives me insane, but it took me years to get underneath that belief system and realize why it's total nonsense.

Yes, it is true that if we perpetuate negative thinking—meaning we focus exclusively on what is wrong—we lower our vibration, and that brings in other lower-vibe stuff. But what has happened through the teaching of the Law of Attraction is that most people have come to believe they need to completely bypass very real emotional processing—and that's something that needs to happen.

That's why this thinking is so harmful. As humans, we are served up loss in all flavors. There are the big losses—the loss of people we love, jobs, marriages, friendships—and everyday losses—time, money, opportunity.

When a loss happens, we must grieve. Grieving is the way that our brains move us through a loss. For smaller losses, the grieving might take a few breaths, but for bigger losses, there is no timeline. When we try to deny our grief experience by "being positive," we're not attracting "better stuff"—we're keeping our energy stuck mid-grief.

Trying to stay positive when you are in legitimate emotional pain is like trying to hold a ball under water. You'll be able to do it for a while, but it takes all your focus, and eventually it will still find its way up.

What I explained to Elizabeth, and what I want you to understand, is that there are two kinds of pain that lead to two very different types of "negative thoughts."

Clean Pain vs. Dirty Pain

The first is clean pain. The second is dirty pain. It is important to understand the difference because clean pain is natural and needs to be felt. Feeling clean pain actually allows in more good stuff, whereas denying or blocking clean pain blocks ease and blessings from entering our lives because we are in full-on resistance mode, pushing against our own truth.

On the other hand, engaging dirty pain is what will attract more negativity into your life. It's critical we know the difference so that we understand how all this works.

Clean pain is the natural human response to loss. Clean pain can look like grief, sadness, anger, even fear. We don't manufacture these responses to what happens; they occur naturally, even in minor situations. Let's say you walk into your local coffee shop and the customer ahead of you snaps at your favorite barista. This barista is someone who always goes out of his way for you, asks how you're doing, is a good person. You may experience anything from sadness to anger to outright rage at witnessing this exchange. Whatever you feel is clean pain, and if you let yourself feel fully whatever comes, it will pass.

You will not have attracted anything negative into your life. Once you've had a chance to feel your feelings, you'll know what to do next. Maybe it will be to give your barista an extra big thank you. Maybe it will be nothing. Either way, if you allow yourself to feel what you are feeling, those feelings will pass.

Dirty pain is manufactured pain. After we've experienced clean pain, sometimes we keep ruminating on the event, using our thoughts to generate more bad feelings. In the coffee shop situation, you processed the clean pain by feeling your feelings, but later that day you decide to think about it again. This isn't a natural emotional response. Your brain pokes you and says, "Remember that jerk earlier?" Rather than emotions leading your thoughts, your thoughts generate your emotions.

You play and replay the scenario in your head, getting angrier and angrier.

You start to tell yourself that this poor barista does nothing but try to be kind to others, and jerks in this world are making life hard on him. You are righteously indignant now—on behalf of this other person. How dare this jerk mess with your favorite barista!

The dirty pain train has now left the station and you are off and running. You are no longer processing a natural reaction to a difficult situation; you are full-on manufacturing negative feelings. These dirty pain feelings are problematic, and you do want to use whatever tools you have to shift your thoughts in a more positive direction. This is the part that Law of Attraction teachings get right—when you are manufacturing dirty pain, you are becoming a "crap magnet" and blocking good stuff from coming in.

But there is a big difference between clean pain and dirty pain, and most manifestation work ignores this critical difference.

In Elizabeth's case, she had been hit with a significant amount of loss in a short time. A few breaths weren't enough to clear all the grief that was coming up. I explained to her how to tell the difference between clean and dirty pain and how to process each type.

Clean pain arrives first, often at the same time as a thought. On the other hand, dirty pain starts as a thought that generates negative emotions.

I told Elizabeth when she was having a good day and felt her mind start to whisper *But you don't have a job . . .* to refocus on something that she liked—creating a painting, watching a comedian on YouTube, or going for a walk.

But on the days when she felt the world sink down on top of her, it was important to breathe into that and let the fears and the sadness flow through.

Let Feelings Flow

Letting feelings flow—instead of pushing them down inside you—can be scary. A question I often get from clients is "What if the pain doesn't stop?" Having two children, a business, and a handful of other people who depend on me, I understand how scary it can be to just let your emotions have their way with you. When a negative emotion like sadness or fear starts to bubble up and it feels really big, it's normal to want to shut it down. I mean, how will you get your son to soccer practice if you are reeling in agony over a lost job?

The reality is that pure emotional reactions don't last very long. We perpetuate them with our thoughts, but the body can only hold an emotion for so long. I find most emotions last about one or two minutes. Initially something in the external world creates a reaction in our nervous system, which generates chemicals that make us feel emotions.

The body will work to clear those chemicals, which takes the minute or two that we are naturally experiencing emotions. If emotions last longer it is because we are now generating those same reactions with our thoughts. Those thoughts then trap us in an emotion spiral where we continue to feel the emotions for much longer than the initial chemical process.

Emotions can feel long-lasting, but if we can stop ourselves from thinking about the situation that caused our emotion and simply feel what we are feeling, we can release the emotion in just a few minutes.

Whether intending to or not, most Law of Attraction teachers have convinced a large population of their students that what they should really do is shove the negative emotions down and slap a smile on their face. This just doesn't work. You can keep the beach ball under the water for only so long. Eventually it's going to pop up—and the more pressure, the bigger the pop.

And all that pressure just creates unconscious resistance that actually blocks the good things from flowing in.

Toxic Gratitude

I've seen this same teaching pop up different ways in many teaching modalities. It's not just the Law of Attraction world that perpetuates it—it's pretty much all spiritual philosophies. I call it "toxic gratitude," and it shows up every time someone says, "I should be grateful."

"My basement is leaking, but I know I should be grateful that I own a home and have the money to fix this problem . . ."

Okay, all true—owning a home and having the money to fix structural issues are true blessings, and appreciating them is definitely a good thing. But repressing the natural, normal negative reaction to a flooded basement is like using your blessings as a sword of punishment on yourself.

All of us—every single human—are going to feel bad from time to time. It is normal. Allowing ourselves to feel those feelings does not mean we are ungrateful or that we are crap magnets. And trying to use gratitude to cover or ignore negative emotions is actually spiritual bypassing.

Spiritual bypassing is the "tendency to use spiritual ideas and practices to sidestep or avoid facing unresolved emotional issues, psychological wounds, and unfinished developmental tasks."[2]

You Aren't "Doing" It Wrong

The other piece of the Manifestation Myth is that if something hasn't shown up, you aren't "doing" the manifestation right. Or more exactly—the myth is that the ultimate proof of "good manifestation" is what you "do" or how you look on the outside.

Time and time again, I've seen people ask a Law of Attraction teacher why, after they've done all the things (visualized, vision boarded, affirmed, etc.), they still haven't received that BMW they wanted.

And the teacher responds, "You must act as if you already have it. You must not be vibrating alignment with this BMW strongly enough." Argghhh! This frustrates me so much for two reasons—first of all, it makes it sound like the Divine is a penal being that has rules that need to be met before She'll deign to grant your wish, like some dysfunctional wizard of Oz.

Second, whenever the key to allowing gifts into our life is tied to "doing" something differently, we are already off track.

What a load of crap! I've had plenty of stuff show up in my life I never dreamed of asking for, and I wasn't acting "as if" I already have them. And I've had quite a few amazing things show up that I doubted I was worthy of, and poof—they arrived.

If acting "as if" was the key to the kingdom, believe me—I'd be hanging out in the moat.

And it's not just me; the graduates of The Receiving School® say the same thing. They came in wanting something to shift in

---

2. https://tricycle.org/magazine/human-nature-buddha-nature/

their life—maybe they wanted more money, a new love partner, to find their excitement for life again—and what amazes them is how much more shows up. Sure, the thing they wanted rolls in, but what blows them away is how things they didn't even know they wanted or needed also arrive—that's the real magic.

Because guess what? The Divine is . . . the Divine. She knows so much better what our soul is truly longing for, what will really bring us alive. And She doesn't need us to walk around life as manifesting robots—acting "as if"—in order to get it.

But She does need us to do one thing—we have to let Her help us. We have to make space for the magic She can create in our lives.

Because She contracted with us to give us free will, and She will never violate that contract. As long as we resist Her help, She will only go so far.

Here is the big takeaway I want you to get from this chapter: however you learned about the way we receive magic, miracles, or manifestation—whether it was originally in a traditional church (like me) or through the modern metaphysical church of self-help and spirituality—it is very likely that somewhere along the way you learned that magic, miracles, and manifestation happen if—and only if—you prove yourself worthy.

If that is the case, you were taught the Manifestation Myth, and now I want you to let that myth go.

You've been worthy of every miracle, manifestation, and piece of magic you could ever desire; the only thing keeping it from you is your resistance. This resistance often happens unconsciously in your brain, but when you come to understand why you hold this resistance, you can learn how to release it and invite that magic into your life.

Chapter 5

The Brain

The way we interact with the world is rooted in experiences and interactions in our childhood. Even the most dysfunctional habits we carry—including the way most of us learned to block magic—are rooted in behaviors we developed as children to feel safe.

You could have had the most idyllic childhood, and there still would have been parts of your experience that made you feel unsafe. As children, we are vulnerable and naturally feel powerless at times. That vulnerability and powerlessness is what leads to issues of safety.

Our brain is programmed to keep us safe, and the part of the brain that is most aware of safety issues is called the amygdala. The amygdala is what fires our fight or flight response. It's designed to get our bodies to behave in a way that secures our physical safety—which often requires that it shut down the "higher thinking" part of the brain in order to take control of the body.

When the amygdala is running the show, it's near impossible to reason your way out of a situation or behavior. The amygdala is the reason why, even when we intellectually understand the Divine is willing to support us and help us, we resist that help. It feels unsafe.

Imperfect Humans Raising Other Imperfect Humans

I clearly remember an afternoon when I was around nine or ten. I had to return library books that were past due. There was a fine owed, so I must have asked for that money. I can't remember whether I asked my mother or father, but I remember my dad exploding in rage that the library books were past due. Our library was just around the corner from our house. We were able to walk there on our own. How could we be so irresponsible?

I don't remember exactly what he said, but I remember how I felt. My heart raced. I wanted to cry, but by then I had learned to shove those feelings down inside me. I listened as he ranted, and I silently resolved to do better, be better.

He was right—how stupid could I have been? The library *was* right around the corner. How *did* this task get away from me? I hated myself.

Although my father did not regularly erupt in rage, it happened enough that I had quickly programmed myself that "getting it right" equaled safety. I'm sure I made mistakes along the way that went unnoticed or were even handled "normally" by my parents, but there were enough blow-ups that mistakes soon equaled danger to my little self.

Having done A LOT of work on myself and this perfectionist tendency, I know that what was really happening in those moments was that my dad was angry with himself. He was frustrated with the mistakes he himself had made, and without a healthy way to deal with them, they just poured out on top of me and my siblings.

He was not a perfectionist—that was my own dysfunctional coping mechanism—but he handed me his own worthiness and self-esteem issues.

In general, my dad was a good man. He was flawed but good. Telling you this story is hard because it paints a single stroke on the life of someone I love dearly who was good to me in so many ways.

But I'm telling you because you may feel you had a "good childhood"—that all in all, you are grateful for the people who raised you. I have found that this narrative keeps people from being honest with the early experiences that caused their dysfunctions.

It feels unfair to "blame" our parents or anyone else for behaviors we still maintain in adulthood when we know better. Here is what I want you to know—you can have amazing, wonderful people love and raise you and still leave childhood with scars.

It's okay.

These childhood scars are a natural product of imperfect humans raising other imperfect humans. If you can be honest about why you are the way you are, it will be easier to let go of those behaviors. Because along the way, you started to reject parts of yourself in order to feel safe, and later in this book I'm going to show you how to invite those parts back in. Bringing your rejected selves back to the party is one of the most powerful ways to release resistance and allow space for magic.

I rejected the part of me that made mistakes . . . which then caused me to develop the "perfectionist" persona. The problem with that identity is twofold: First, I'm human and therefore not perfect, which means I make mistakes and am never able to feel whole. Second, great success only comes with a willingness to fail. My avoidance of failure kept my dreams very small for a very long time.

But the good news is that we can shift this at any time. All this dysfunction and self-misunderstanding is housed in our brains, and our brains are malleable. We can change the way we think and work.

The Fear Brain

But before we jump into reprogramming our brains and inviting back in all our rejected selves, let me explain how the amygdala causes you to hold onto dysfunctional behaviors long after you've learned they aren't helpful.

The amygdala is this tiny almond-shaped part of the brain. It's basically the control center that's in charge of responding to stressful events. Its job is to decide whether we are facing a dangerous situation, rate the level of the danger, and redistribute resources to respond to the situation.

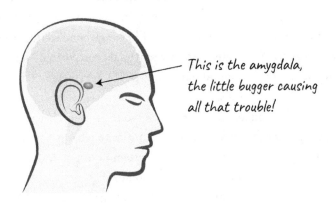

This is the amygdala, the little bugger causing all that trouble!

The amygdala is often referred to as the lizard brain, but I like to think of it more like a grizzled old war general. This guy's job is to know when to move troops, to know when to send missiles, and to constantly have a strategy for defense.

This part of your brain has one mission and one mission only: to keep you safe. That's good, right? It is—as long as it's been programmed to understand what real danger is.

Unfortunately, from a young age, we've been taught to interpret normal, naturally occurring events (like late library books) as dangerous events.

Did you even see the move *WarGames?* In it, high school student David Lightman (played by Matthew Broderick) hacks into a military supercomputer while searching for new video games. After starting a game of Global Thermonuclear War, Lightman leads the US military computer system to believe it's being attacked by the Soviet Union, which starts a counter-response. In reality, the Soviet Union is not getting ready to attack the US, but the system believes that is the case.

That is what happens to our amygdala in childhood. Because we don't have a full understanding of what is really happening, a situation feels dangerous and triggers the body to release stress chemicals that tell the amygdala, "This is dangerous." The amygdala is not an emotional center; it's a programming center. It registers the event (and its interpretation of the event) as "dangerous" and will now respond to that event accordingly. So, in my case, my amygdala categorized "returning library books late" as dangerous AND interpreted making a mistake as dangerous.

At the end of *WarGames,* everyone is saved because the main character is able to alert authorities to what is happening, and they reprogram the computer system to interpret the events differently, aborting the counter-response.

Like this computer system, the amygdala has one job and one job only: to help you survive. Every minute of every day, it is scanning the environment, looking for threats to your survival.

The amygdala's carefully orchestrated yet near-instantaneous sequence of hormonal changes and physiological responses help you fight off a threat or flee to safety. Unfortunately, the body can also overreact to stressors that are not life-threatening, such as traffic jams, work pressure, and family difficulties.[3]

As long as your amygdala equates "needing help" as dangerous, it will use a complex system of brain commands to keep you from allowing Divine support in. Your logical thinking brain can understand that getting help is a good thing, but if childhood experiences made you feel otherwise, your amygdala will remain in charge.

Most of us learned at an early age that being "needy" was bad, so we rejected the "needy" part of ourselves. Later on, we'll talk about how to start accepting the part of you that needs support and learn to trust that those needs will be met.

The Fiction We Live By

Alfred Adler, founder of individual psychology, theorized that our memories of our life are not accurate. We have a story line that defines what we believe our life has been like, and we retain the memories in a way that supports that plot. In essence, our memories are more fiction than fact.

I first encountered Adler's work in my second semester of graduate work for a master's degree in psychology. Adler's take on why we do what we do and the way we do it—even when those actions don't seem to support a healthy outcome—made sense of behaviors I had never understood before.

Adler's theory was that as children, we interpret events without full context and write a script that is essentially fiction (e.g., making mistakes is dangerous). We then filter events,

---

3. See https://www.health.harvard.edu/staying-healthy/understanding-the
-stress-response

conversations, and relationships through this fiction in a way that strengthens it.

For example, once I had that "making mistakes is dangerous" fiction in my head, let's say I made a mistake in school and a teacher met that mistake with compassion. Even though she showed me that it was perfectly okay, even important, to make mistakes along my learning journey, I would immediately "lose" that memory because it didn't fit with the story I had learned to tell myself. But if I dropped my milk walking back from the lunch line and one person laughed, I might blow that memory up to include the entire cafeteria making fun of me.

As I continued to work through my master's program, I took as many classes as I could with the professor that first introduced me to Adler. I didn't know it at the time, but his words would direct everything I did later in my career as I developed The Receiving Method™ and established The Receiving School®.

At the start of each semester, this Adlerian professor would have the entire class memorize exactly one key sentence: "Everyone is doing the best they can with what they have." On every test he asked us to repeat this one Adlerian mantra.

It was the precursor to the idea that "people who know better, do better."

Right now, I want you to embrace this mantra as well. It will free you from a ton of criticism of yourself and also help you access compassion for the people around you. We are all operating from an individualized "guiding fiction." What doesn't make sense in the cold light of "truth" or "reality" always makes sense through the filter of our guiding fictions.

Later, when we discuss how to start receiving the parts of ourselves we rejected, you'll have access to a process that allows you to write a new fiction for yourself. For now, I want you to hear this: You are doing the very best you can with what you have.

Becoming Fit for Society

Before we move on, I want to introduce you to one other psychological theorist who helped me understand childhood and its effects on the brain and our behavior. His name was Carl Rogers, and he posited that we are always reaching for self-actualization (the top of the Maslow Hierarchy of Needs) but that most of us don't get there because we aren't given an environment to thrive.

He believed we all had the ability to reach our greatest potential, but a particular environment was necessary in order to do so. To achieve self-actualization, we all need three things:

- genuineness (openness and self-disclosure)
- acceptance (being seen with unconditional positive regard)
- empathy (being listened to and understood)

Rogers believed we all have unique endpoints in our potential, meaning the greatest version of you is unique to you and likely very different from me or anyone else. He also believed that the knowledge of how to become the greatest version of you rested inside you and only you.

If this is the case, your natural instincts and reactions are perfect for your ideal life growth. You are born with a compass guiding you to your north star of self-actualization, and no one else has access to that compass but you.

Sounds beautiful, doesn't it?

When I first encountered Rogers's philosophy, I had just given birth to my daughter and was raising my two-year-old boy, who had some instincts and behaviors that were not exactly a good fit for gentle society.

He didn't like to go to bed, often found himself so consumed by love for his baby sister that he squeezed her tighter than a newborn should be squeezed, and thought it completely appropriate to throw things.

Basically—he was a normal toddler.

Using Rogers's approach, I understood that all my son's behaviors were meant to be received with unconditional positive regard. As an exhausted mother of two littles, I thought Rogers was an egotistical male who never had to raise an actual child himself.

I liked what he had to say but only to a point. I did not (and still don't) believe that a child would need to be raised with unconditional positive regard in order to self-actualize. I did, however, believe he had a lot to offer on how to create an environment for ourselves to self-actualize—one that countered the goal-driven banking environment I was in.

I had always been a fairly transparent manager and mentor, but I started to lean into Rogers's teachings a bit more. I chose to see all my team members through Adler's lens of "everyone is doing the best they can with what they have," and I tried to reach to challenges in a person's approach or behavior by first listening to their explanation. As I regarded them with acceptance and respect, I noticed immediate shifts in their behaviors.

At home, I tried to offer my son the same rules of engagement (genuineness, acceptance, and empathy), but it was much harder. As a parent, it is very difficult to stay in the present moment with a child. It's so easy to jump into the future. As much as I wanted to be fully accepting of my son, I feared that acceptance would ultimately turn him into a social reject. As he threw his food on the floor, I thought about ignoring or focusing on something positive, but my fear-brain kept producing images of a twenty-something man with no friends or job, a social reject because he couldn't manage to keep his food on his plate (among other troubling behaviors, such as screaming when something didn't go his way).

I found myself constantly weighing the risks of hurting his self-esteem with raising a sociopath.

I share this story simply because it's easy to look back on the way our parents raised us and blame them for dysfunctional coping behaviors we developed. But the reality is that even our parents were doing the best they could with what they had.

I was armed with a slew of psychological theory, financial stability, and a full parenting partner—and yet most of my parenting was dictated by a fierce mama-bear need to help my kids succeed, which apparently weighed heavily on the side of making them "fit for society."

Every parent screws up. Yours did. Mine did. I did, and if you have kids, you probably did too.

It's okay. We can still create an environment for ourselves that allows us to reach our full potential—to thrive, feel excited about life, and treat this crazy journey as an adventure.

Even though our human parents may have screwed up a little—or a lot—we have always had a Divine parent who gave us the genuineness, acceptance, and empathy Rogers said we'd need for self-actualization.

We just missed it because we were so busy paying attention to the noisy humans in the room.

Chapter 6

Your Wake-Up Moment

You may be wondering—if the brain works so hard to keep us fixed in resistance, how does anyone break free?

Well, the answer is simple: the brain is just not as powerful as the Divine. The Divine is always conspiring to ensure you can achieve the biggest version of the greatest vision of your life. Yes, you have free will, but you also have a metaphysical team working really hard to keep you on "your path."

They can't force you to stay on your path, but they can make it very hard to stray too far off it.

Let me explain why that is.

Before you incarnated in this particular human form, you existed in a place or dimension that held no resistance. You might call it heaven or something else, but in this place, all your needs were met.

You didn't need to wait for anything—manifestation was instantaneous in this plane. Actually, manifestation was unnecessary, because your very existence was so peaceful and expansive that true desires—money, things, support—were unnecessary. You were free from fear and encompassed by love.

Think of living in a place with the exact same beautiful weather every single day. Eventually you would desire contrast—something different.

That desire for contrast is what led you to incarnate.

In preparing to become incarnate, you chose a personality and life circumstances which would allow you to experience the kind of contrast you desired. And this contrast was meant to expand as a soul and bring your unique light to the world.

You gathered your team of Spirit Guides around you, looked down at planet Earth, identified a specific type of darkness that your light was a match for, and said, "This is my place." Once you knew that, you got to work picking the personality traits, family of origin, community, and anything else you'd need to walk the path you wanted to walk.

You might see that people with learning challenges have trouble loving themselves or accepting themselves. Your purpose might be to bring compassion to that population. If that is the case, you would likely choose to have a learning challenge yourself. How else would you truly be able to reach someone who feels so alone in their journey but by joining them?

Depending on the unique lessons you wanted to experience, you might choose parents who rejected you for your learning challenge or parents who completely accepted you and easily saw your light.

Although in the human form we would certainly see those "difficult" parents as "worse" from a life purpose perspective, if you chose them, they were the very best parents to help you bring your light to the world and to learn what you came to learn.

How the Universe Guides Us

Before you jumped into your human form, you, your Spirit Guides, and the Divine all agreed on a few things:

1. You would forget that you are an extension of the Divine, capable of creating anything and everything you chose, completely loved and worthy at all times. The reason you'd want to forget all this is because without it, you'd never really be able to experience what you wanted to experience.

2. The Divine and your Spirit Guides would ensure that you encountered any experience or person you absolutely had to encounter to fulfill your mission on earth. For example, if there was a teacher who would show you how to learn in your way, you would absolutely have that teacher, even if your parents wanted to move, she wanted to retire, etc.

3. You would have free will, which means you might veer off your path. But if you did, your "team" would send you signs to get you back on your path.

Those signs would come in three ways.

At first you would get gentle nudges from your team. These would show up as whispers of intuition, a stranger saying something unexpected in passing, a movie plot that wakes you up to a new way of looking at things.

If those nudges didn't work, you would then get a whack upside the head. (Don't judge—this is what you wanted; you knew how important it was to follow your path!) Let's say you had a friend who wasn't good for your path. At first you might feel a bit uncomfortable when with them. If you ignored that feeling, you two might be caught unexpectedly doing something you shouldn't, and you would get a wildly exaggerated punishment. (Maybe your team would inspire your parents to ground you for a month—the whack upside the head.)

If the nudge and whack didn't work, your team wouldn't give up—they would move on to the boulder on the head. The boulder feels like just that—overwhelming, crushing, unfair. But in reality, it's the most loving way for your team to protect you from something far worse in the grand scheme of your life—you heading too far off your path.

In the unhelpful friend scenario, let's say you ignore your gut and deal with the punishment—but continue to be sucked back into this person's world. Your team can see that if you stay in that person's life, you will wander far off your path and end up lost and alone on that journey. They don't want that for you, so although it won't feel good, they will do whatever it takes to wake you up.

You might end up in a store with your friend where they suddenly commit a crime. You have nothing to do with it, yet you end up arrested and in jail. It will feel so unfair. If you understood what angels and Guides were, you might even wonder—where are they? How'd they let this happen?

And the answer is that they didn't just let this happen—they made it happen. Because your night in jail is a way better outcome than you sitting in a crappy apartment, ten years later, having dropped out of school and wondering how you got there.

The Divine, our team, is always conspiring on our behalf. And they wanted you to find this book. They wanted you to wake up to the support you have access to. They see the potential waiting for you, and they want you to have it all!

Right now, there is something you want to change in your life. It might be a relationship, a career move, a financial situation, or just escaping a general feeling of blah-ness. You've probably already gotten a nudge on what to do next (or maybe this book is it).

You might have gotten a whack. You might have even gotten the boulder. Wherever you are on your journey, just know what has happened has happened *for* you, not to you.

If you can embrace that one idea right now, things will get so much easier.

The faster you learn to heed those nudges, the fewer boulders you'll find in your path.

Wendi's Story

Take Wendi, the client I told you about in chapter three. She loved her career for years. If you'd asked her during those years, she would have said she was definitely on her "path." But as the world changed and her daughter grew, she found the hours and responsibilities felt heavy.

At first, the idea of heading out on her own and launching a consulting firm felt exciting. (That was her nudge.) But each time she'd get ready to leave her stable income, she got scared.

She'd step back from the ledge of the leap she knew she needed to take.

She convinced herself that the "responsible" decision was to keep her guaranteed salary. She loved her team, and it was really just her hours that were a problem, she told herself.

Then her company was bought out and she lost her job. (You might think that's the boulder, but that was only her whack.)

Wendi made a small attempt to get some private clients while out of work, just to tide her over while she continued to scan LinkedIn for other jobs and sent her resume out. Eventually she got an offer, and she jumped at it.

She quickly found herself in a much worse place—less pay, worse hours. She slogged through tough hours to collect a paycheck that no longer lit her up.

Each week she got whack after whack telling her that she should leave, but she hung on. (Our team usually will give us quite a few whacks before they resort to a boulder.) Then COVID came, and she was let go. And as her industry went through a massive collective downsizing, there were absolutely no job opportunities anywhere.

That terrible series of losses on so many levels was a massive boulder for many people—Wendi included.

All her security was ripped away, leaving her with exactly one option—to start her own company. And all this happened on the back of losing her dad.

During this time, Wendi often asked me why this was happening and why it had to be so hard. That was reasonable. She was a good person, had lived her whole life with one focus—to help her family and the customers she served. What did she do to end up here?

I told her what I'm going to tell you: if something in your life is making you feel the same way . . . you did nothing wrong. You are here because these are the exact circumstances that will create the highest version of the greatest vision of your life. You are here because you may have missed a few nudges along the way—and you may even have ignored the whacks. But all of those happened to serve one purpose, the same purpose a boulder serves: to help you find your way back on your path.

Your team can't force you on your path; you have free will. But they can make it excruciating to stay off it.

The good news is that once we heed the whisper, the whack, or the boulder, we also have our team's limitless support in achieving what we truly want. And when we choose to do this and make space for magic to help us, we start to have lives we only dreamed were possible.

Everything Told Him to Quit . . .

Years ago, my husband, Matt, worked in an incredibly high-pressure job. He had endless nudges and whacks that told him to leave. At night, I'd look over at him and could tell he wasn't even there. The stress was too much. A few times I suggested he look for another job (after all, sometimes our team will use the people we love to nudge us). But he never did. This particular job had been a huge leap in pay and status, and I think a part of him doubted anyone else would extend him the same opportunity.

Eventually the boulder came. Matt's nose broke out in a rash. At first we didn't think anything of it, but it quickly spread. Within forty-eight hours, it covered the entire left side of his face around his eye. He saw his dermatologist, who quickly diagnosed him with shingles.

Like most people, we thought shingles was something that appeared on the torso, but the doctor explained that a small portion of people get it around the eye and sent him to an eye doctor.

Things quickly escalated. The ophthalmologist (who had been seeing patients for forty years) said Matt's case was the worst he had ever seen and that Matt was at risk for losing his sight in that eye. But the bigger scarier message was this: the reason Matt's shingles got this bad, this fast was due to stress— and most men would have died of a heart attack long before this could happen.

Talk about a boulder. Matt was stuck in bed for weeks with a painful condition that was constant proof of the level of stress he was under. But, like Wendi, the desire for a "good paycheck" kept Matt going back, even though he had proof that his job was literally putting his life at risk.

Eventually, like Wendi, Matt and most of his colleagues lost their jobs during a massive industry downsizing. We were heading into the recession of 2008, and Matt ended up out of work for two years.

Although those two years were really hard on us for many reasons, I'm so grateful he got that boulder. We are celebrating our twentieth wedding anniversary soon, and for that fact alone—that he is alive and well to celebrate it with me—I'll take the boulder.

And what I can tell you for sure is this: no matter how painful these boulders in your life are, when you get enough distance from them, you'll be able to see the gift. Once you learn how to create space for magic, you'll also see how easy it is to just put them aside and create what you truly want.

By the way, these nudges, whacks, and boulders are not arbitrary or violent. They are the last resort—the most loving way to keep us truly safe. The nudge happens when we are about to walk into something far worse and there is no other way to stop us. Someone had already screamed "stop," but we kept going. The whack and eventually the boulder are the kindest ways our metaphysical team has to guide us back to a course correction.

Part II

Opening

Chapter 7

My Story

All these nudges, whacks, and boulders have a singular purpose: to teach us surrender.

For control freaks and perfectionists like me, surrender is as close to a curse word as I know. For us, our safety is centered in exactly one place: our ability to get things done, to make things happen, to fix, to heal (others).

Surrender means letting go of what we have come to believe—and the world has taught us to believe—is our superpower.

Any good self-help or spiritual course will have surrender at its foundation, and yet as much as I have spent my life studying spiritual principles—first in Catholic school and then on the path I am on now—I have not come across the "how to surrender" process anywhere. It is because the "how to" part is so elusive that the Universe offers us the nudge/whack/boulder approach.

Later in this book, I'm going to give you what I believe is as close to a "how to" on surrender as a human can get. But the reality is, unless you've experienced a few boulders over the head, it is unlikely you would even have the desire to keep reading.

Surrender is a lesson I can't teach alone; we can't truly appreciate the lesson until the Universe has laid the groundwork. The

Universe nudges and whacks us not to hurt us but to wake us up to a truth She begs us to understand: control is not in our hands, however much our reality may try to convince us otherwise. Only when we let go, when we surrender, can help from the Divine flow in. The Universe has our backs always, and She is determined to make sure we know it.

If the Universe has already opened your heart, then the "how to surrender" lesson will be much more valuable to you.

My Boulders

What I most hope is that this book has caught you before you've had to be hit too many times over the head. I also hope that I've been hit over the head enough for both of us—for all of us—and that you can learn from my boulders.

Like any determined, accomplished woman, I needed to get hit pretty hard, pretty often before I found my way here. Never was that truer than the two years that encompassed my mother's cancer diagnosis and ultimate death.

When I remember myself during those two years, what I see is a woman who was so desperate to fix everything and save everyone that she lost herself. From this vantage point eight years later, it's so obvious what I "should" have done. It's so obvious how I could have made life so much easier on myself by creating space for the magic I so desperately needed, but the risk in surrender (I believed) was too great.

The Doctors Found Something

"The doctors found something."

The day my mom told me she had cancer can be told in two ways—from the perspective of the person I was then and the one I am now. If I tell it from my current perspective, you'll see everything I see now—and the lessons will be so obvious. And yet it wasn't obvious to me then. I was so consumed in a chaotic fog that picking out the pieces of truth was difficult.

I had just left my position at the bank and was riding high on the fumes of the unrealistic optimism that come in the early stages of entrepreneurism. I was taking courses and learning and playing at being a business owner without facing the actual real work—marketing, sales, and business planning.

My husband and I were outside in our cul-de-sac as our children played. My son rode around and around on his little bike while we pushed our daughter in a plastic car. It was mind-numbingly boring to be out there—going around and around—but the day was beautiful, and I was trying to drink in the sun and the fresh air.

I suspect what I really wanted was to be back inside on my computer, dreaming up new stuff about my business, things like logo, colors, or names—the stuff that new entrepreneurs believe matter but are secondary to the real work.

Although my memories of that day are something of a blur now, the only thing that remains crystal clear is the image of my parents walking toward the cul-de-sac, having parked a few spots down on our street. Looking back, I can now see I heard the first whisper—the message meant to wake me up.

Whispers, when understood, help you prepare, to remind you to open to the help of the Universe. When we don't understand them, we swat them away like annoying gnats.

My whisper at that moment was that my dad was standing next to my mom as they walked toward us. My mother dropped by all the time to see her favorite people (her grandkids), but my dad rarely joined her. Although my dad was the first to get down and play with the grandkids when we visited him, he was just a homebody and that was that. So when I saw them both walking toward us, something buzzed around the edges of my brain, something that said, "This is different. This is important."

After the kids got their hugs and kisses, my mom asked if she could talk to me—alone. Whisper, whisper, whisper . . . I told her, "Sure!" and Matt took my kids and dad inside.

Suppressing Our Truth

In that moment, I would have told you I didn't suspect anything. But looking back, I can tell you that I was using a tremendous amount of energy to ignore all the warning bells going off deep down inside. For those with toxic independence, the ability to take a stress response and turn it completely to the "mute" position is a pretty normal strategy.

We take every emotion that could possibly need anything from us—fear, sadness, overwhelm—and place it in a box, a box we've learned to keep tightly shut. So although I would have told you I had no idea what was coming, the truth is, my body was saying, "Warning! Warning! Something really hard and scary is coming—bring in reinforcements!" But when we've learned to rely only on ourselves and lock all our needs up on a box, we make it impossible to access the help available to us.

With all my warnings locked tightly away in a box, my mom told me that when the doctors had taken a scan of her shoulder after a recent procedure, they had found something.

(I have come to loathe those words. My mom was the first one to say them to me, but I have been through so many journeys with people I love that have started with "they found something" that I can genuinely say those words suck.)

I don't remember much else about that day, but here is what I do remember. In that moment, as my mom told me she had lung cancer, I know she was ready to hold me. She was ready to open her arms and hold my pain. She was ready to be my mother. And I couldn't let her.

I'm not sure I could even access the little girl who needed that hug that day. I had put her away so long ago—and learning to find her would take the next two years.

I was ready to move onto details, planning, learning what we could *do* to fix this.

She asked, "Are you okay, Patty?" Her eyes were searching for the pain she knew was there and unable to reach it.

I couldn't let her in then, but eventually that changed. Two years later, knowing she wouldn't be alive much longer, we often sat talking. I was able to drop fully into those conversations because by then all the nudges and whacks and boulders from the Universe had finally accomplished some of what they were trying to do.

After two years of trying to save my mother—intervening on her behalf, researching treatments, advocating for care, and running on empty most of the time—hitting roadblock and disappointment over and over again—I finally learned to surrender. I used every ounce of my energy trying to save my mother, but ultimately, I had to face the reality that there was no amount of DOING that would change the course of her life.

So many times over those two years, I received nudges and whacks telling me I was not powerful enough to influence the course of my mother's life. But it wasn't until I received the boulder—the truth that my mom was dying and I had a few months left with her—that I finally let go.

I let go of trying to save her and accepted I just didn't have that power. Once I was able to allow what was happening to happen, I had to face the pain—but I also experienced the magic.

I Locked My Voice Away

In one of those conversations toward the end, my mother confided that when I was young, she would look at me and know I was in pain, but she had no way to reach it. I was so shut down, and she wasn't sure how to get in. She told me sometimes she would beg me to tell her what was wrong, but I wouldn't let her in. I don't remember that part.

We can have parents who love us and want to help but still lack the resources—mental, emotional, financial—to help us learn to safely surrender our needs to them.

If I had learned to open up and allow help much earlier on how, I'm not sure how I would have handled that moment my mother first told me she had cancer.

I know for a fact she didn't come there looking to be held; she came to hold me. One of my regrets—that rests in a library of little regrets on our path together—is that I prevented her from mothering me right then. I know now that's what she truly wanted—to help me while she could. But I was so busy moving into "fix it" mode that I missed it all.

It's unlikely that I would have broken down crying, but maybe I would have. The needs of the people I love still factor into everything I do, even now that I understand the process of surrendering and letting go on a much deeper level. So I probably wouldn't have wanted her to see me cry.

But I think I could have at least accessed an honest answer— "I'm not sure if I'm okay. I think I just need time to process this." And then I would have let her hold me. Later on, when I was alone, I would have let it roll over me—all the pain and fear.

Instead, I immediately shoved all those sticky emotions back into the box and sealed it tight.

"Fear, pain, and worry are things for people who don't believe in what is possible!" I would have said. Already having been brainwashed by the spiritual dogma of toxic positivity, I would have believed the best way to keep my mother alive was to BE POSITIVE!

I don't know what words I used in talking with my mother, but I know what I communicated: "We'll figure this out." And what I meant was, "I will make you better. I don't care how much of my energy I use up doing it. I will fix this, and I will be your savior. I will put what I need on hold until you are well."

Of course, the real problem with that last promise—which many of us unconsciously make—is that it isn't just a promise; it's a contract. There is an unspoken expectation we don't realize we hold, which is "and when you are well then I will finally be able to let go, and you will take care of me."

The problem is that waiting for every one of us to be "okay" before we allow our needs to be met leads us in a constant cycle of waiting for that time and becoming more and more numb, overwhelmed, and lost in our own lives.

Nudge, Whack, Whack, Boulder—Thump

The years following that first conversation served up a number of whacks and a few boulders. I'm sure there were hundreds—if not thousands—of nudges, but I think I've even filtered out some of the less painful whacks.

Looking back, I can see how clearly the Universe was conspiring to teach me to let go, begging me even, like my mom used to when I was a kid: "Let us in!"

But there I stood holding it all in, holding it all together, just not feeling safe to let go. It's amazing how much we buy into our own illusions of safety—misunderstanding what keeps us truly safe.

The first few months after my mom's diagnosis were particularly rough. It had been determined that she'd need lung surgery and likely chemo, but the chemo would be decided based on the results of the surgery.

Right before the surgery was scheduled to take place, my mom fell and broke her hip. They were able to pin it, but post-surgery the pin slipped, and she was in constant pain. Even so, the collective team of doctors determined that a hip replacement (which would have been the answer to her pain) would push out her lung surgery too far. The risk was too great.

My mom opted to deal with the pain in favor of faster cancer treatment.

The added complication for me was that although we had many people willing to help transport my mom to appointments and treatments, my minivan was the only one that was the right height and structure to give her any comfort.

I couldn't bring myself to hand her off to anyone else, knowing that she'd be in more pain because of it.

That is often our motivation for keeping so many people's plates spinning for them—we know how much it will hurt them if they drop, and we can't bear to see them endure the pain. That was certainly my motivation.

As the summer went on, I became more and more disconnected from myself. The more I tried to be there for my mom, my kids, and everyone else who needed me, the more I lost track of myself. Of course I did, because had I stopped for a moment and felt what I was feeling, I thought I would be swallowed up by the tsunami of emotions I had buried inside.

To me, keeping those emotions shoved down deep inside equated to keeping my mother alive.

Even in the blur of my memories, there are a few whacks that stand out to me.

When my mom was first at rehab after getting the pin put in her hip, I was visiting her. I was the only person she'd let stay very long. She told me she couldn't stand to see the pity on her friends' faces—it was too much.

So between trying to grow my struggling new business, watch the kids (I had reduced their day care hours to two days a week), ignore the fact that our income didn't really equal our bills anymore, and a few other plates that were spinning, the soul inside me was quickly getting lost.

I was barely in my body.

The First Whack

So the Universe sent a whack. Backing out of my parking spot at the rehab facility, already thinking about the client call I needed to get to and wondering if I could wrap that up in time to pick my son up from preschool, I hit another car.

It wasn't a big hit, only a gentle whack (as whacks go).

Even so, I got out of the car and saw I had dented the other car. My heart started to race. I had no idea where the owner of the car was to exchange information. I ran inside the facility, but no one there had a good idea on how to track someone down. I borrowed paper and wrote the owner a note.

I told them how sorry I was. I told them I knew they were probably visiting someone they loved right now, and I felt terrible knowing I might have made their day worse with my accident. I gave them my phone number.

I felt horrible—horrible for causing damage, horrible for bringing an expense to our family when I wasn't generating anywhere near the income I had generated in the "safe" job I had left. All I felt in the middle of all this was "not enough." But in reality, the Universe was begging me to hear "slow down!"

As the day went on, I silently prayed for help.

Later that night my phone rang—it was the owner of the car. She told me she got the note but said it was really no big deal. She was pretty sure they'd be able to pop the dent out. No, she didn't need my insurance.

I couldn't believe it. It was the first time I felt grace in that journey—the ability to find peace in all the mess. I knew the Divine had answered my prayer, but I confused the answer. I thought the Divine had helped take the financial burden off my plate, and She had. But what She was really trying to say was, "I can help with anything! Let me in!"

At the time, money was quickly becoming a stressor. I was unable to focus on my business the way a new entrepreneur should and unable to focus on the important work when I did have time, and it was leading me to a very unprofitable business. I was scared, but I couldn't admit it.

I had never had a problem making money. I convinced myself this was all because of these "lack" feelings. This latest miracle strengthened my resolve to have faith! And trust! But that was in a singular focus—toward money.

Having faith and trusting that my mom would be okay without my constant vigilance was not something I was willing to consider.

Over the next two months, I caused damage to our van three more times—the first two happened pulling out of our garage, scraping the paint job as I went. This was a large garage I had pulled in and out of thousands of times, but suddenly I couldn't maneuver it. I ignored those whacks. But the last one happened as I pulled into a parking lot to attend a networking event and backed the van straight into a wall.

Looking back, it's almost funny to think how hard the Universe was trying to show me how out of it I was. For the most part, I didn't get it. That last one I did take as a sign—a sign that I better DO BETTER when I was driving. *What if my kids had been in the car?* I thought. Again, although the Divine was just trying to say, "Patty, look at yourself! You need help!" all I heard was, "Pull yourself together and be MORE!"

Boulder Day

Finally, the boulder came a few weeks after that last accident. By that point, I was beyond exhausted and stressed. I headed out in the morning, happy that the one thing I allowed myself to have help with—cleaning my house—was about to be done. My cleaner, Eliza, was such a gift, always kind and gentle.

When I walked back into the house later that day, I immediately knew something was wrong. I couldn't quite put my finger on it, but as I walked through the first room, I realized Eliza hadn't been there. Nudge, nudge, nudge.

A part of me I had lost access to understood something was wrong, but I had long since silenced her.

"Hmmmm . . . Maybe I got the day wrong? What day is it?" I thought as I headed to the answering machine I saw blinking. We rarely got messages. I figured it was Eliza letting me know something had come up—that she needed to reschedule, although she had never done that to us in the three years I knew her.

I was surprised to see I had not one but three messages.

I pressed play.

The first was a friend of mine—she was sobbing, asking me to call her and not to look at the news until I did.

The second was my husband's doctor. He said the biopsy was back and that we needed to talk.

The third was Eliza's stepdaughter. She asked me to please call her.

I wish I could remember what I was feeling at that moment. I felt terror, I know that—terror mixed with numbness. It's a weird combination.

And I also knew the terror wasn't coming from a normal place. It was still the same voice that said, "You are not enough! You are not enough!" I felt like I hadn't kept enough plates in the air and now they were crashing down around me—except I didn't even know what plates they were.

As I called each person back, I soon found out.

A father in our community had been killed the night before by a drunk driver. His son was one of my son's closest friends at the time—as much as a three-year-old has close friends.

My husband had cancer.

Eliza, who was exactly my age with two small children similar ages to mine, had died suddenly of a brain aneurysm.

These were some serious boulders. I am not suggesting that each of these situations was created as a boulder for me—simply that the Universe arranged it so all the dominoes fell at once for me, making the avalanche so big I couldn't look away.

I think I spent most of that day crying. And after that the crying came easier.

I wish I could tell you this was enough to tip the balance and help me understand that my well was on empty, that life was short, and to let go a bit. To a certain extent, that did happen.

But this was more like one of the boulders I can now look back on and point to and say, "Oh yes, look there—that was one of those days where the Universe stepped in with a boulder-sized response to my numbness said, 'Let some fucking help in, you lunatic!'"

The Next Two Years

Over the next two years, my mom finished her treatments, got a successful hip replacement, and had over a year of clean scans.

I got my business sorted out and launched an actual brand with a business plan the following year.

At the same time, I launched my new business—literally the exact same day my husband lost his job and was out of work for two years.

The next year, we learned my mom's cancer was back.

And with a growing but still new-ish business and a husband out of work, our savings shrank and eventually our debt grew to levels that choked us.

Through all of this, there were exhilarating highs—the first clean scan, the first birthday without cancer—first my mom's and then mine. Matt's cancer ended up being a blip on the radar. Even the layoff felt like a blessing at first, having already received warnings in the form of shingles that his job was killing him.

There are a lot of exciting moments when you are launching a new venture, and each of those was fun and adventurous, almost outweighing the lack of income that came with a promise of future income.

And there were more bonks on the head.

Here is what I've found. It takes a lot for us humans to wake up to our own self-imposed limitations, the lies we tell ourselves that keep us disconnected from who we truly are, what we truly want, and the space for the magic that can bring that to life.

Luckily for me, when it came to my mom, I finally learned to surrender before it was too late.

Almost three years after that first conversation when my mom told me, "They found something," I was sitting across from my mom's oncologist when he said what I knew but didn't know.

"The chemo isn't working. It's time to consider palliative care."

We refused hospice at first. Of course we did. My mother and I both share a rock-solid faith in miracles. But I finally stopped believing I was the miracle.

I didn't want hospice—not because I was still fighting against the truth, but because a very real truth was that she could still get better. I knew it was unlikely, but I also knew the Divine could make this happen if it was for my mom's highest good.

That being said, for the most part I flowed with what was available. Healers, green juices, Reiki were all brought to the table. I never stopped wanting my mom to get better, but I did stop thinking I was the one that could make that happen.

True Surrender

Two years of whacks and boulders had finally taught me to surrender.

I was present in our relationship. I was present in my pain. I still didn't understand how much help was available to me or how to ask for it, but I stopped denying how much help I needed.

I stopped trying to fix my mom and just dropped into a state of being with her.

One morning I walked in, and when I looked at her, I knew. I knew she had decided to leave. She didn't look remarkably different than she had when I visited her the day before, but I felt it. I felt the truth of her soul.

Being able to see this is one of the gifts of letting go. When we stop refusing our needs, our emotions, our*selves*, we start receiving all the truth we hold inside us. This was one of those truths. I knew my mom had decided to go.

I didn't say anything to her. I just sat there, feeling the truth of the loss. Feeling the pain. Feeling the joy that I could still hold her hand.

She was nodding off as she often did, and I could tell she needed to sleep. I asked her a few times if she wanted to take a nap, but she insisted she didn't. Finally, I said, "Mom, why won't you go nap? You're so tired."

She answered, "I don't want you to leave. I want this time with you."

"So let's take a nap together."

The Book of Love

When I look back on the journey with mom through her cancer and death, this is my very favorite moment ever.

My mom lay down in her bed, and I lay next to her. There was an exquisite level of peace around us. Maybe it was the simple joy of resting or something else, but I remember just loving that moment so much.

I held my mom's hand. I have always loved my mom's hands. When I think of my childhood, I see my mom's hands, stirring cake batter, applying lotion, reaching to hug me. Everything that was good in my childhood included those hands.

I thought about how much I loved those hands as we lay there quietly.

She asked me to talk to her, so I did. I asked her the question I had been wanting to ask her since I realized she probably wasn't going to be with us much longer.

"Mom, is there anything you wanted to do that you never got to do?"

My mother had put everyone in her life first. I suspected there were a few dreams left unfulfilled because she had spent so much time taking care of others.

She answered quickly, "Oh! I never wrote my book!"

My mind whirred. A book? I had never heard her mention a desire to write a book. I'd never seen her write more than a birthday card or a recipe card in my entire life. An ache started to fill my heart. My mom had this big dream to write a book and now it was too late.

I knew it! It felt so unfair that she had spent her life caring for others in such a big way, loving so many, and now she was dying with this dream left unrealized.

"What book, Mom?"

"My Book of Love," she said simply. "The book where I tell you and your brother and your sister how much I love you. How much I have loved being your mother."

That was her regret, that she had not written down what she showed us every single day of our lives. Her regret was simply that she wouldn't have a way to keep reminding of us of her love after she was gone.

I kissed my mom's hand. I didn't say anything. It didn't matter that I already had all the memories that would have been written in that book. It didn't matter that I knew that love story by heart. I let my mom cradle that regret because it was hers.

My mom's regret made me smile, because it opened up a world of knowledge about my mom and also what it looks like to live a full life.

I had always wondered if my mom ever felt like she lost out because she had spent so much time taking care of us and our extended family. But she didn't. Her only regret was that she didn't have a way to love us more or for longer.

My mom had fulfilled her life purpose: to love. It was that simple. And as I watched her drift off to sleep, I looked at the hand I still held, the hand I loved so much. The hand that had given me five million caresses, the hand that had baked hundreds of cakes and thousands of cookies, the hand that had always smelled of Vaseline Intensive Care lotion.

That is when I realized that hand belonged to a woman who did not miss out on anything because of the way she loved. That hand belonged to a woman who had the privilege of leaving the world with a single regret—that she couldn't love more.

And that is the moment when my heart broke open to a single truth: accolades and achievements are wonderful and fun, but a successful life will never be defined by what we achieve or how famous we become. A life's success will be defined by how big we have loved.

Right now, nine years later, I still have many moments days (or weeks) where I wonder if I am doing enough, creating enough, being enough. When that shadow of doubt starts to wrap itself around me, I use that day with my mom to bring me out of it. I just think, "How can I put more love into the world today?" And whatever answer my soul gives me, I know that is my north star to success.

And when I think, "How can I let more love in?" that is my north star to happiness.

I wish I could say that when my mom crossed over a few weeks later I had learned to surrender to love fully. That isn't true. In fact, I'm still on that journey, but I've learned a few things along the way, and I want to share them with you so that you don't have to walk the path I walked—feeling numb or lost inside the business of your life.

When you learn how to receive all the love and support available to you, your life will start to change. Challenges will dissolve, money will flow in, life will get easier. Your experience of the "material world" will improve. But that isn't the greatest gift here.

Every day, you write a page in your own book of love. I don't want you to miss a single sentence. At the end of your life, the material world will no longer matter, and the moments of love and kindness are all you will take with you into the next life.

It's important to learn to release overwhelm, debt, or even boredom—but even more important is this: release whatever keeps you out of each moment.

My great aunt lived in a nursing home at the end of her life. She needed constant care. We all wondered how her poor body hung on for so long when it was so clearly ready to go. But a nun who visited her daily told us, "You have no idea what blessings a life holds. Every breath is a prayer."

Let Go and Receive

It took me an awful long time and a LOT of pain to get to this place of awareness. I don't want you to think this is what your journey needs to entail—but if you don't learn these lessons sooner than I did, your journey may include pain.

Of course, your wake-up moment doesn't have to include the death of a parent or loved one. I hope it's as simple as waking up one day and feeling the pain of your current life and wanting something better, something easier. Answer the whisper, and you'll never feel the whack.

What I've found is that if we choose to ignore the call to let go—the call from the Universe to surrender—the whisper will turn to whacks and the whacks to boulders, every single time.

Your journey probably won't look like mine. I tend to make things pretty hard on myself, and it always seems to take me a really long time—with lots of missteps—to learn lessons. But the upside is that once I'm done, I'm able to teach those lessons to others in a way that is much easier, less painful, and far less time consuming.

The Receiving Method™ was birthed out of these lessons I've learned. My hope is that a whisper brought you here and that you'll learn what the Divine most wants you to know without any whacks, without any boulders.

Here is that message: You are loved. You are cared for. You are worthy—always. You always have support, and all your desires can and will be met if you do one thing:

Let go and receive. That is what creates space for magic.

Chapter 8

Understanding Our Limits to Asking

I wasn't the only one who struggled to allow in help and support through my mom's journey through cancer. My mom did as well. In fact, watching her helped me see what I was doing myself.

In the first part of her cancer journey, it was incredibly difficult for her to ask for or receive help. She hated being a burden, and she made that clear over and over. I understood that.

But by the time the cancer came back—and certainly when it got to the point that she had very little mobility—her resistance to help dropped away. What was the point? The closer she got to exiting this world, the more her perception of her own "burden" on others disappeared.

For me personally, it was much easier to help her when she was open to it than when she was always trying to do it "by herself." I started to see that this need to do it "by myself" had been passed down to me.

The last month of her life and the months after she passed gave me time to reflect. I saw how hard I had made this journey on myself, and I saw that this was something I was taught to do.

My mom never meant to teach me this, but I absorbed it from watching her.

We are all designed to be relational beings. In the healthiest form, being a relational being means we see our interconnectedness and act from that place. But we have some holdover programming from thousands of years ago that distorts what being relational means.

Back when humans could only survive in tribes, our interconnectedness drove different behaviors. In order to survive, each person played a role in the tribe, and you had to stick with your role in order to stay a part of the tribe.

If the medicine woman suddenly decided she wanted to be a hunter, that didn't work very well, because when hunters came home wounded, there would be no one to care for their wounds. And the reverse was true as well. If a hunter suddenly decided her job was tending the fire and making clothing, the tribe would end up with less food.

The tribe survived if and only if people played the role assigned them by the tribe. If you didn't play your role, you risked being thrown out of the tribe. A person without her tribe would not have been able to survive, and so the need to be accepted by the tribe was programmed into our deepest level of survival.

Even though we no longer live in a time and place that requires the tribe accept us in order to survive, our fear brain—the amygdala—still acts as if this is true. From a young age, we work at figuring out what makes us "acceptable" to our tribe and build on what we perceive that is.

Typically, your family of origin is your original tribe. Once you start to go to school, you expand your "tribe" to include peers and eventually, society at large.

As you move through stages of your early development (first as a toddler, small child, teen, etc.), you adjust yourself to become more and more acceptable without even knowing it. Sometimes, what each of those groups wants from you to be "acceptable" is very different, leading you to take on different personas based on where you are and who you're with.

But there is one commonality in all these groups you spend time with and are a part of—and it has to do with asking and needing help. Consistently, we are taught that asking for and needing help makes us needy, weak, undesirable. Doing, achieving, fixing, helping is what makes us desirable.

This happens in our homes, our schools, and our workplaces.

You can grow up with the best parents who fostered you to be incredibly curious and made it absolutely safe to ask for help—but if you observed them always doing it "by themselves" and never asking for help, that is the example you will try to live up to.

We don't teach our children who they are by how we treat them; we teach them who they are by how we treat ourselves. Our children's model for what a fully functioning member of the family "tribe" is comes from the adults in the family.

Heal Yourself, Heal Your Child

When The Receiving School® members start to understand their dysfunctional or problematic relationship to asking for and receiving help, they often ask, "How can I help my child open up to greater receiving?"

The answer is simple: "Do the work yourself."

If you have children in your family line—whether they are your own children or nieces, nephews, or close cousins—you have the power to shift the trajectory of their relationship with what it means to ask for help.

A healer once taught me that when we heal something in ourselves, we heal it seven generations back and seven generations forward. I have since heard this principle revisited in many ancient traditions, and it's the one that gives me the greatest comfort.

I can tell you for sure that my mother's own shift in relationship to asking for and receiving help was a huge door-opener for me. And I've watched this in my own family. This doesn't just apply to asking for help; it applies to all family wounds—worthiness, lack, sufficiency, addiction (the list is long).

When we do the work to release our wounds around something toxic—something that blocks us from having a full and open relationship with ourselves, the Divine, and the world at large—we heal it for our lineage.

If you are worried about a child, the most powerful thing you can do to help them (besides loving them fully exactly as they are) is to heal your own stuff—plain and simple. And the most powerful wound to heal is the wound that asking for help is bad.

When I get tired of doing my work on these issues (and that happens more than I would like it to) this is the motivation that keeps me going. This, to me, is the true legacy I can leave behind, that I did what I could to heal my children and my children's children.

That I lifted the curse that we inherited unconsciously over so many, many generations, and in doing so, have gifted my ancestors their own freedom.

Asking is the key that unlocks the door to our personal freedom, abundance, and self-acceptance. When we learn to ask—without fear or resistance—we step into a level of power unknown before.

Asking Made Simple

Now that you know that asking is the key that unlocks the door to EVERYTHING, I bet you're ready to get ASKING!

But know that there is a lot of misinformation out there in the spiritual and Law of Attraction worlds about how to ask.

In fact, almost everything you have learned about how to "get" the Divine to provide for you has focused on how you ask. In some circles, they might call it "how to manifest."

When I first started learning about the Law of Attraction, I was immediately smitten. The idea that it didn't have to be so *hard* excited me. I learned how to create a vision board, and I'll admit—the first time I made one, it was fun.

I was told that by creating a visual representation of what I desired, I would "call it in."

The only problem is that not everything showed up. As I discussed this in Law of Attraction circles, what I learned was that I needed to visualize more—really see myself already having it.

So I did that.

And I did it some more.

I visualized like it was my job. Some of the items on my vision board showed up in truly miraculous ways, while others didn't show at all.

I continued to ask the question, "What am I doing wrong?"

The Law of Attraction community I belonged to was eager to give answers. I was directly or indirectly told I wasn't doing it right or doing it enough. The recommendations were to do more: more affirmations, more visualizations, more vision boards, more living "as if."

It wasn't until after my mom's death and later my dad's death that I unlocked the truth about why these methods only worked so far and then stopped.

I was missing a piece of the puzzle.

The Missing Piece

The truth was that all of these methods are designed for one purpose—to ask the Divine to fulfill a desire and to call that desire forth. The only problem is that I didn't know how to *receive* all those gifts once they arrived.

You can do all the "manifesting" you want, but all that will do is bring what you desire to your doorstep. If you don't know how to open the door, it won't matter how good you are at manifesting.

In all this manifestation work, I was being taught how to *ask*, but I wasn't being taught how to *receive*. The reality was that like every human out there, I carried resistance to receiving easily, and until I learned to release that resistance, it didn't matter how elaborate my asking was.

I've already started to discuss how to release resistance, and I'll continue to discuss it. But what I want you to understand right now is that asking doesn't have to be as hard as I made it or as hard as you are probably making it.

In fact, when we make "asking" difficult by putting elaborate work into "manifesting," we actually increase our field of resistance, keeping what we desire just out of arm's reach.

As I dove deeper and deeper into the world of the Law of Attraction, I actually started to feel like there was something wrong with me. I was missing the "special sauce" that made someone a good manifester.

Yes, I actually did have a lot of wonderful things show up, but much of what I desired was still out of reach. I was putting all my energy into asking, when really what I should have been doing was *relaxing and letting the Divine take over*.

Whatever word you use for the "Power" that provides for us, I think we can all agree that the Power is all-knowing.

The Divine doesn't need an elaborate vision board to know what is in our hearts. The Divine is beyond time, space, language, sight—so why would we need to ask a certain way or do a certain action in order for Her to know what we desire? She doesn't.

My breakthrough moment came a few years ago when my dad passed away suddenly, and the truth about how all this work was revealed to me. The year he died I did very little to "manifest" anything—and yet amidst so much grief I also saw beautiful gifts flow in, in ways I never could have imagined before.

You'll learn more about that story later, but the point is that so much of what I had wanted for the longest time came to fruition in that year and I did absolutely nothing to make it happen.

There were no vision boards, no affirmation, no living "as if." Yet things I had asked for previously started to flow in, as naturally as a wave returning to shore.

Once I connected the dots that the real work wasn't in asking or "manifesting" but in receiving, I let go of all those gyrations once and for all and simplified my asking process to something so simple you can do it right now.

When a new desire fills my heart and I'd like the Divine's support in bringing it into my reality, I simply ask.

Ask—and that's all you have to do.

You can whisper your ask.

You can write it down.

You can scream it.

You can think it.

You can daydream it.

Whatever feels good to you is what feels good to the Divine.

And there are no special ways or special tricks to do it. You don't have to feel it as if it's already here. You don't have to write it in the present tense as if it's the moment in time that you are receiving it.

Think about it—do you really think an omnipotent force who loves you as Her own child requires that you ask a special way before she'll respond to you? Or that She'd favor Her other children that learned a special way to ask over you?

Is that what the Divine most wants for us?

If your child came to you and wanted your help, would you only respond if they asked in a specific way, if they came to you with an open heart? Of course not! As parents, we *want* to help our children. The Divine wants the same.

Ask. Ask. Ask.

The key is to ask.

The one limitation to this process is that you do have to actually ask. I know that might seem obvious, but as I've run trainings to thousands of people, I've found that many times people limit what they ask for.

There are a lot of reasons for this, but the biggest limitation I see in people is that they aren't 100 percent sure what it is they want. So without having all the details, they don't ask.

Here is more good news: the Divine understands us deeply. As long as we can own that we want *something*, She can fill in the blanks on everything else—even if we aren't 100 percent sure how that looks.

If I asked you, "What will make you happy?" and you're like most women, you might say "a nap" or "time alone." But when pressed about what would create long-term lasting happiness, you might say, "I don't think I even know anymore."

I get it. I got lost along that path myself. Caring for my people, juggling financial obligations, and life in general changed me. By the time I was in my late thirties, things that used to make me happy lost their luster.

It's okay if you've lost track of what you want. You have pieces of the puzzle, and if you own those pieces, the Divine can fill in the blank.

Do you know you want to feel healthier? Want to have more fun? Would love to find a new love or friend? Ask for that!

You don't have to know the details for the Divine to start to fulfill those desires. In fact, I found the more open we are to what we receive, the better it gets.

From Paralegal to Pastry Chef

That's exactly what happened to Joanna when she took a training I offered last year on releasing blocks to abundance. During the training, I walked our participants through a process to open up to more help from the Divine.

At the end of the training, each person had homework: write down exactly what you want. As part of the training, I showed Joanna and the other participants how to move into "receiving energy" to allow those desires to be met. (Don't worry; we'll do that in the next section.)

At the time, Joanna was an underpaid legal secretary. She had obtained additional training as a paralegal to give her a bump in salary, but after completing the training, her boss kept her at the same low pay. She said she was "unfulfilled and making $12 an hour."

Joanna wrote, "I want a job that will help me be independent, where I can be creative and use my talents to grow."

She thought she was asking for a better paralegal job with a different boss, but what she got was so much better!

A few weeks after taking our training, a job for an assistant pastry chef appeared in her social media feed. She was a talented baker but had no formal training. Even so, she applied and—drumroll—got the job.

The pay was great, and the hours gave her plenty of flexibility to be with her kids—something she didn't even think of asking for. She told me this was so much better than anything she could dream up for herself. Fast forward a few months later, and the pandemic hit. Like most food service businesses, her boss knew they had to let staff go and only had space for one pastry chef.

To Joanna's surprise, her boss let the head pastry chef go and promoted Joanna.

Now Joanna makes even more money, with greater freedom to flex her creative muscles, and she is ridiculously happy doing something she loves that she had no idea she was even qualified to do.

"I have better pay, better hours, full benefits. I am appreciated. I am respected. I work in my own kitchen, make my own hours. My boss trusts that everything I make will be good. I'll be getting an assistant shortly."

It really is that simple. Own what you want. Ask with an open heart. Any desire your soul can create, can be met. You are already worthy of the gifts you most desire.

The Divine would not let you hold a desire that could not be met. THAT is law.

Chapter 9

How the Divine Responds

You're probably wondering, "If asking is the key—exactly how do I ask? Because Patty—I feel like I've already been asking, and I don't seem to be getting what I want!"

That is a very good question!

Let me start by saying that if you asked for something and it hasn't arrived, a few things could be going on. What you've asked for has arrived just outside the door of your reality, but because you are still in resistance it isn't able to show up inside your reality.

I am going to cover how to release that resistance in later chapters.

What can also be the case—but is much less likely—is that you asked and the answer you received was, "No, this would not be for your highest good."

The Divine will not allow a desire to be met if it is not for your highest good—or if it would be better for you to arrive at a later time.

This is often the case when we ask for a magic wand to erase a major difficulty in our life that we are meant to learn from. Until we learn what we need to learn from it, the Divine will not remove the challenge because She understands how important this lesson is to your life journey.

Divine "No" vs. Lottery Winning

You often see this in the case of lottery winners. A huge sum of money comes into their lives and ultimately leaves it, often leaving them worse off than they started. If the lottery winner has not learned what they need to learn to exist in a state of abundance, the money cannot stay.

I'm convinced some of these beautiful people took on the journey of winning and losing large sums of money to help all of us understand that large sums of money fix very few of the things we believe they will. And if we don't create the space for that money to remain, it will not stay.

Take Janite Lee, who won $18 million in 1993. Eight years later, she filed for bankruptcy. This is certainly not the only rags-to-riches-to-rags story out there, but this is also such a good example of why a Divine "no" can be better than if She said "yes."

Ms. Lee didn't squander away her money; she actually gave most of her money away. In fact, she gave more than she had to give. Her lottery winnings went to supporting the Democratic Party and charitable donations, including having a law library named after her.[4]

Ms. Lee wanted to help others, but she had never learned how to honor balance and flow. Because she had not learned how to receive, the increased money that came into her life only amplified the effect of her imbalanced relationship to giving and receiving.

I know a lot of women who tell me that the reason they want more money is not for themselves but so they can take care of others. This is wonderful—to want to help others—but if we don't learn to factor ourselves into our own receiving equation,

---

4. https://www.businessinsider.com/lottery-winners-lost-everything-2017 -8#janite-lee-spent-it-all-on-charity-and-political-donations-16E

we will remain out of balance and that imbalance will only be amplified when money does come in.

Have you asked for a large sum of money from the Divine (or any big miraculous gift) and felt your request was ignored? If so, what would change if you knew that your request was answered but the answer was a loving "No, not yet"?

If you knew for certain that this desire had not yet been met because something better was coming from the delay? What would that mean?

I can tell you from personal experience that a loving "no!" is a wonderful gift, but it often takes time to actually view it that way.

The Truth about Debt

A few months after my mom passed away, I was walking in the cemetery where she was buried. This was something I did almost daily after visiting her grave.

The initial shock that accompanies early grief was starting to wear off, and reality was setting in again. My company was still not making the kind of money I knew I was capable of bringing in. Matt was still out of work, and our debt was growing.

I started talking to whomever was listening on the other side of the veil—my angels, Spirit Guides, the Divine. "Why is this happening to us? We are good people! I did everything right! I left my job to follow my *calling*. Matt always worked hard. I took care of my mom—I was there for her ALL THE TIME!

"And what do we get for it? All this debt! It's so unfair. You tell me why this happening—why after all I've done for others, after I have been good and loyal to everyone I love and built an entire business to HELP PEOPLE—why am I left with a broken heart and this crushing debt?

"What did I do wrong?!" I demanded.

I was sobbing. Every part of me hurt—my heart from the grief, my mind from trying to find the answer to a problem I couldn't solve, and my body from all the stress. I felt abandoned on every level—and I was angry!

I couldn't figure out why the Divine would not lift the burden of debt off us when we had given so much.

Just then an energy floated in and around me. It's an energy I've come to understand as angels. Their energy is always softer than most of my Spirit Guides, who tend to be much sterner with me.

They said, "You haven't done anything wrong. This is not a punishment. Debt is simply the result of giving more than you have to give. It's time to take care of yourself. You need to learn how to receive."

WHOA!

(If you'd like help connecting to your Spirit Guides and Angels I've provided a meditation to help you do just that here: www.PattyLennon.com/MSFMresources)

The tears continued to roll down my cheeks, but that one message sucked the anger out of my body. I think deep down inside I believed I really had done something wrong to create all this debt. I believed that I hadn't been enough. I hadn't been responsible enough with our money. I hadn't been "enough" of an entrepreneur. Someone different would have been able to juggle growing a business, encouraging a husband who was struggling, raising two small children, and caring for the mom I loved with every cell of *my* body while she slowly faded from *her* body.

In the entrepreneurial space I was deeply immersed in at the time, I was constantly absorbing the message that "good" entrepreneurs succeeded because they hustled and had grit. Up until that moment, I was convinced this was the reason we were so in debt—because I didn't have enough grit.

It would take a few more years before I completely saw the "grit and hustle" messaging as a symptom of the dysfunctional ego-led energy of the entrepreneurial space. One that left very little room for feminine wisdom and magic. But right there in that cemetery, that angel message created enough space for me to consider a different perspective, and that different perspective helped me ask for a different kind of help.

Right there I said, "Please help me not to give more than I have to give. Help me learn to receive."

The good news is that the Divine never abandons us. She might say "no" to completely fixing the problem we are struggling with, but She will always supply us with all the help She can along the way. When we don't see something showing up that we've asked for and suspect it's because we've been given a Divine "no, not yet," the key is to revise what we are asking for.

If the Divine had said "yes" to my request to free me from my debt, I would have lost out on some powerful gifts along the way.

When those angels gave me that message that day, I started to embrace my debt as a symptom rather than a tangible thing. If you had a physical symptom, like a stomachache, you would look at what was causing the pain. You might say, "Divine, please free me from this pain," but more likely you'd focus on changing something to relieve the pain. If the pain was strong enough, you'd definitely shift behaviors.

You also wouldn't think, "Agh, I am a bad human. I created a stomachache." You'd likely see that something your stomach needed was missing—less acid, less fiber, less stress, etc.

That's what the angels helped me do. I slowly learned to stop seeing the debt as my "fault" and instead saw it as the natural result of an imbalance. And so I turned my attention to creating balance in my giving and receiving.

And this doesn't just apply to money requests.

When someone enters The Receiving School®, I ask them, "What do you most want to get from your time here? What is a tangible shift you'd like to see that will show you this 'receiving stuff' is working?"

One of our members, Debbie, said, "I want to be loved and cherished."

Debbie had been caring for her sick husband for some time, and she was also raising two children. She felt unloved and underappreciated. She wanted it to be different.

Each week, she'd do all the exercises but report in that her husband wasn't acting any differently. I gently offered that needing another person to change in order for us to have what we desire isn't possible.

The Divine will not change another person to suit us. The Divine can create conditions for each person involved to be their best self, but the Divine will never force any of us to change. We must choose that.

But even when another person doesn't change, our desires can still be met. We just have to be willing to let them.

Six months later, Debbie reported she and her husband were separating. His illness had started to resolve itself, and as he got physically better, he decided he wasn't happy in their marriage. The truth was that he had it pretty good. Debbie did all the heavy lifting in the home, so for him to choose to leave the marriage was a big step.

Debbie said she was very hurt at first, but then she came to realize that this was exactly what she needed. She never would have had the courage to leave her husband, and yet the Divine gave her husband the courage to make that choice for them.

After her husband moved out, Debbie said she suddenly felt free. She loved herself more, and that love and appreciation she was looking for was really meant to come from within. Without her unhappy, constantly complaining husband, she suddenly saw how amazing she was and how happy she could be.

I know the deep romantic love Debbie is seeking is on her way to her. But before any of us can receive that kind of love from another, we have to be able to give it to ourselves. Debbie now understands what the Divine most wanted her to know, and she's in a position to receive even greater things.

Chapter 10

Understanding Resistance and How It Shows Up

Another big misconception in the Law of Attraction community is that attraction is a focused effort. If you want more money, you do things to bring money in—you have conversations with money and tell it how much you love it, or you write yourself big checks the Universe is meant to cash (à la Jim Carrey). If you want a romantic partner, you sleep on one side of the bed or clear out half your drawers to make room for them.

There is nothing wrong with doing any of these things, and in fact, I've seen them work for people—but not for the reason they think.

If writing a check to ourselves for $1 million was all it took to call that money into our reality, I think we can all agree that a lot more people would have $1 million in their bank account.

Most people take these efforts because they believe the effort is actually calling what they want to them (the check for $1 million is drawing $1 million to them). In reality, the reason any of this works is because it helps the brain get on board with the idea that it could be true.

When this happens, the brain stops resisting Divine flow and essentially opens the front door to let the manifestation in. If it is for your highest good, the Divine starts flowing that $1 million to you as soon as you desire it. You don't need to write a check to make that happen.

But if She sends you the money, you have to actually open the door to let it in. Most of us have our doors shut to abundance of every kind, and that door is what I call resistance.

Even when we start to understand, "Oh, I must be doing something to block this abundance," it becomes difficult to figure out exactly what it is we are doing. We've been guided to focus on specific actions around the specific form of abundance we want, which just complicates things.

There is only one door.

We don't have a money door, a love door, a health door. Yet everything we are taught in the manifestation space acts as if we do. If we want love, focus on bringing love in. But what the manifestation world doesn't teach is that if your general field of resistance is strong, it doesn't matter how many drawers you clear out of your bedroom. It will be really hard for the romantic partner to get through.

I didn't fully get this until seven years after my mom passed away and my dad died suddenly.

After that day in the cemetery with my angels, I started to approach our debt differently. I looked at where I was giving more than I had to give—especially when it involved money. And things started to improve.

By the time my dad passed, we had released a big portion of the debt that had been weighing us down, and our financial situation was much better. But the year after my dad passed—despite feeling the loss of my dad almost daily—our outer lives got significantly better on all fronts, including money.

And what I learned in that year is what led me to create The Receiving Method™ that I'm sharing with you now.

Failed Launch and Lessons

I loved my dad deeply, and when those police officers showed up at my door to tell me he had passed, it was like the rug was pulled out from under me.

On that day, I had been readying myself for a big launch in my business. In fact, we were supposed to "open the cart" the next day. Opening the cart is something you do when you are going to put a program on sale for a short period of time and ultimately "close the cart" a few days later.

Prior to "open cart," there is a marketing launch. In my case, my marketing launch consisted of a series of training videos that introduced people to my work. Statistically speaking, our launch was doing really well. We had hundreds of people engaged in the training, and those numbers told us that we would likely have a six-figure launch, but you never know until the cart actually opens how many will buy.

The launch itself lasts about ten days, and during that time, the excitement for what is being released builds up. That excitement is what drives sales, and by all accounts, people were excited.

For some entrepreneurs, it might have been a difficult decision not to "open the cart" the day after someone they love dies. A lot of time, money, and energy goes into a launch, and if you don't harness the power of the excitement that has been built up, you lose all the power of that time, money, and energy you invested.

For most of us, we only launch a couple of times a year, so each one counts.

But the program I was launching was a mastermind, which meant whoever joined would get my focused attention. I knew what the grief journey was like, and I couldn't in good faith ask people to invest in me when I wasn't sure I had 100 percent to give them.

I had my business manager send an email to everyone who had been watching our trainings. We had a final training scheduled on open cart day, and she told them that my dad had passed and that I would be unable to deliver that final training and announce my new program. She told them I would open it as soon as I had time to grieve.

The people in our community were amazingly loving. I felt terrible about leaving this last piece of the launch puzzle out of place, but everyone just said they'd be ready when I was ready.

From a business perspective, this was like flushing $100k down the drain, but I knew it was the right thing to do. I needed to grieve in order to be able to serve my clients later on.

Two Months of Freedom

I gave myself two months. During that time, I put most of my energy to opening wide to stay connected to my dad. I had the ability to talk to my mom after she crossed, and I knew the same was possible with my dad—the key was staying open.

All my priorities fell away as I walked through each day receiving whatever greeted me. Sometimes it was a message from my dad or my mom. Sometimes it was a deep wave of grief. And every once in a while, a big burst of joy would fill me up—the most surprising gift of all.

Eventually I felt ready to complete the training I had started during the launch and open our cart. I had absolutely no financial expectations. Like I said, most sales come as a result of that excitement "pressure system" created during a launch, and all that pressure had long since disappeared.

To my total surprise, we ended up with $82,000 sales over the course of five days, and an additional $40,000 came a few months later as a result of the same marketing.

That year was the most financially profitable in my business history. But it wasn't just the money that made me pay attention. As hard as the grieving was, I felt the most connected to myself as well as my community. I experienced the greatest level of love and support I had ever had.

About six months after my dad died, I was sitting by our pool. It was the last days of summer, and I was relaxing and thinking about everything that had transpired up until that point. Suddenly it hit me.

It was so obvious, I couldn't believe I hadn't seen it before.

Resistance isn't specific to certain types of abundance. We don't have "resistance to money" or "resistance to love." Resistance is a force field, and it was a force field I had just spent six months releasing.

In my effort to stay open and receive everything that was coming (so that I could grieve and receive communication from my dad on the other side of the veil), I had released my resistance to *everything*!

The Field of Resistance

In that moment, I saw resistance as what it truly is—a field that exists around us. And that field is either thin or dense.

Yes, I had released my debt slowly since that day in the cemetery because I started to understand debt in a new way. But the real reason I released debt was because I had learned to focus on balancing what was going out with what was coming in. That had caused me to release resistance, and that lower resistance was what allowed the resolution of our debt to find us.

Wheels and gears in my mind started clicking into place. Because of my background in psychology and study of brain science, I had known for a long time that allowing ourselves the room to feel clean pain was important. We all feel bad from time to time, and it's not mentally healthy to try to suppress true emotion in favor of the toxic positivity mentioned earlier in this book.

Over the years, I had helped people relieve stress and become more successful in part by giving them permission to feel their feelings. But I didn't understand the full impact of what was happening until that very moment.

When we deny our feelings, we aren't receiving them, which creates resistance. The resistance blocks abundance and works against us. When we start to allow ourselves to feel our feelings, we receive them and thus lower resistance.

The theories I had fallen in love with while doing my master's in psychology—Rogers's and Adler's—started to make sense in a whole new context. When Rogers said that we need unconditional positive regard (a.k.a. acceptance) in order to reach our fullest potential, it wasn't just because that makes the mind work better. It was because full acceptance eliminates our resistance.

When Adler posited that "everyone is doing the best they can with what they have," he wasn't just talking about a way to better mental health. That idea leads us to stop fighting who we are (and who others are) and, as a result, live without resistance. In turn, this allows the most abundant "guiding fiction" of our lives to flow through.

Our greatest source of resistance is not to money or love or anything outside ourselves. Our greatest form of resistance is to ourselves. We resist who we truly are and, as a result, block all the gifts the Divine sends us.

Resistance as Self-Rejection

At its heart, this self-rejection or resistance comes from two false beliefs:

1. The Divine judges us and doesn't always love us.
2. We are not enough.

These two false beliefs cause us to lock parts of ourselves away in our efforts to become more acceptable to our "tribe" and ultimately to the Divine. To free ourselves from this trap, we must ultimately accept ourselves and then the world around us.

During those months after my dad died, I gave myself 100 percent permission to be whoever I was at any given moment of the day.

Enough time had passed after my mom's passing that I saw how I could have made that journey so much easier. I understood the landscape of grief and knew I couldn't make the difficult emotions go away by forcing myself to be any way other than what I was.

I also knew if I let myself flow with what came up, I'd be able to ride the waves of grief with much more ease.

This grounded sense of peace and happiness I was experiencing—despite being steeped in loss—was a direct result of receiving myself exactly how I was, and the ripples of receiving energy emanated out from there.

In that moment by the pool, I knew I had found the key that unlocked the door—the door that kept every gift the Divine flows to us just outside our reach. The door was resistance. The key was releasing resistance.

What is so amazing in all of this is that we don't have to have focused attention on releasing resistance. In fact, it is usually harder to release resistance around something we are really attached to. But when we focus on releasing resistance in something less triggering, we lower the entire field of resistance, and everything improves.

Abigail's Story

Take my client Abigail. For the longest time, Abigail never felt financially stable, despite her company's success. She told me that when she had a $20,000 cushion in her business account and a guaranteed flow of business, she'd "feel" secure, but not until then.

As I intuitively tapped into the resistance Abigail was holding to greater financial flow, what I felt was that she didn't have the capacity to handle more flow and needed to bring on team members. In the past, Abigail resisted bringing contractors on because she wanted the work to flow in first to guarantee their salaries.

We agreed the Universe would never flow her more business than she could handle, so if she wanted that additional flow, she'd have to get the help first.

Over the course of three months, Abigail did the work to bring on more help and start to structure her business to hand work off more easily. The more she let in help, the greater the ease she felt. Focusing on *receiving* support and working on the fears that came up when she did allowed her to release a tremendous amount of resistance.

At the end of those three months, she was shocked to see that the business flow that was starting to come in was double what it had been before—without changing anything in her sales and marketing. AND she had a $20,000 cushion in her bank account.

When we put our energy into releasing resistance in any area, *every* area improves!

Symptoms of Resistance

You may be wondering where you are holding resistance or even how much resistance you are holding. The symptoms are pretty easy to spot once you know how to look for them. The key is being willing to see the truth of your situation.

I, for one, used to be able to ignore symptoms until they became critical. Before I share some of the symptoms of resistance, I want to tell you a story of how denial works and what it looks like.

Twenty years ago, I almost died. I didn't have a near-death experience, in case that's where you think I'm going with this. In fact, if the doctor didn't tell me I almost died, I would have had no idea.

At the time I was a true Type-A banker. I worked long hours and pushed hard. NOTHING could stop me. I was known to be a "get 'er done" kind of person.

The day before I ended up in the hospital "almost dying," I thought I had a stomach bug. I canceled a meeting and went to bed early. (That alone was very unusual for me.) Early the next morning I woke up in excruciating pain and was running a fever. By the time I got to the emergency room bed, I was dehydrated, delusional, and near unconscious.

The nurses and doctors hooked me up with antibiotics, painkillers, and fluids.

Once I was coherent, the doctor told me that had we gotten there even thirty minutes later, I would likely have died. I had a severe kidney infection and sepsis had already set in.

He also said there was absolutely no way I had not had symptoms telling me something was wrong. As he reviewed what I likely experienced leading up to that day—back pain, fatigue, nausea—it was obvious he was right.

I had experienced all that and just worked through the pain. I used Advil, caffeine, and dry toast to get me through the days, thinking it would pass. Tolerating discomfort had become a natural part of my people-pleasing, perfectionist nature—and it almost killed me.

Just like your body, your soul also gives you signs and symptoms when something isn't right. But if you are like most loving people who are focused on trying to get through their massive to-do list and take care of their people, you've probably learned to work through the discomfort that is telling you something has to change.

The symptoms you may be seeing that are telling you something needs to change are

- Overwhelm
- Exhaustion
- Absence of fun
- Anxiety
- Lack of resources (like money, time, energy)
- Sadness

Or, worst of all, numbness, feeling nothing. If you are at that last stage of numbness, you've **shut yourself completely down to avoid the pain** that is trying to show you the way out.

The answer to relieve these symptoms is to learn how to redefine selfishness and release your resistance to receiving.

Redefine Selfish

Remember how Abigail originally had such a hard time bringing in the support of other contractors? She feared that if she brought them in before she had sufficient client contracts, she'd end up "wasting money" on those people.

In her mind, it would be irresponsible to "spend" money on help if she wasn't sure she could make money in the process. This belief system put her in a catch-22, because without the help in place prior to client contracts being signed, she couldn't feel good about bringing extra work, and the Universe responded to that resistance.

Even though she was working eighty-plus hours a week and needed the help, her mind kept telling her she'd be taking money from her family if she did this. She'd be selfish.

As people go through The Receiving School® and start to uncover the source of their resistance, a majority report that their resistance comes from a fear of being selfish. They believe if they release their resistance, which opens them to more receiving, others will suffer.

This idea of "selfishness" is at the root of most beliefs that cause resistance.

Most people stay in resistance because in order to release resistance, they have to let go of the responsibility to take care of others and let go of their worry about what others will think.

Each day as we walk through the world, we unconsciously reject ourselves. We reject what we want, what we need, and what we know in favor of what others want, need, and know. This self-rejection is at its heart the strongest form of resistance we hold.

In the next section of the book, I'm going to show you different ways to open to receiving, but the truth is that if you simply received *yourself,* your world would fall into place. That is easier said than done, however, because from a young age you've been taught to reject yourself, and you've come to equate that as safety. I know that sounds crazy, but it's true. What is even crazier is that we teach others (even our children—especially our children) to reject themselves too.

Abigail was exhausted. She knew she needed help. It was obvious. But paying for help (in her mind) would decrease the profit in her business. She had learned at a young age that a good person is someone who works hard and does it herself unless it is absolutely necessary to get help. She had also watched her father invest significant amounts of money in a business that ultimately failed financially.

This "hard work" value—matched with a fear of financial failure—caused her to reject the part of her that was screaming for help.

However, as she refocused her attention on what her intuitive voice was telling her, she opened up to bringing on team members to support her.

Now she has a team of five doing the work she never wanted to do, and she gets to focus on the design work she loves. Her business is growing at warp speed, and she has a huge amount in savings.

She says what is happening now always felt possible, and yet there was always a block she couldn't quite see. Now the block is gone, and she's excited for what is possible.

3 Types of Resistance

You may be wondering what else creates resistance. The three ways we create resistance are by

1. Resisting or denying what is happening outside ourselves.
2. Rejecting ourselves.
3. Refusing the help the Divine and our metaphysical teams are sending us every day.

In order to release our resistance and receive at greater levels, we have to understand the way we create resistance and actively shift our relationship to our outer world, ourselves, and the Divine.

We can do that by following the Five Rules of Receiving that are the basis of The Receiving Method™.

Part III

Receiving

Chapter 11

The Five Rules of Receiving

The Five Rules of Receiving are guideposts that show you where you might be creating resistance. It is natural to want to reject or ignore these guideposts, but I have found that they are the simplest way to understand where your resistance lies.

They are

1. Receive the Outer World
2. Receive Yourself
3. Clear Space to Make Space
4. Learn Your Language
5. Do Your 100%

Rule #1: Receive the Outer World—Even the Ugly Parts

After I had that conversation with my angels in the cemetery and they helped free me from the shame I held around our debt, the debt didn't instantly disappear.

When I shared this cemetery story with my community, one of our members asked what I did to release that debt.

I know why she asked—she wanted to know, "What are the steps that will get me out of debt?" And the answer is—it is different for every person. But one of the key shifts I made was to stop resisting my debt.

Tapping into how I really felt about the debt helped me connect to some important emotions, but there was still more I had to look at. Namely, we had been playing the credit card shuffle with our debt, which kept me from knowing exactly how big our credit card debt was.

We would take out 0% credit card offers, move a balance, and when that 0% interest rate was getting ready to expire, I'd move it to another card. The problem was that we took out multiple cards, and although I might know how much was on any particular card, I never knew how much it all added up to.

My strategy was to keep the debt serviced by paying the minimum monthly amount owed, the idea being that at 0%, I'd be paying the balance down. The only problem was that we didn't always have enough 0% options to cover all our debt, and sometimes balances would spend three, six, even nine months at a much higher interest rate.

Using my Law of Attraction teachings, I would do all the things to make the debt go away—symbolically burn the debt, send gratitude to the banks that trusted me to take this debt on, visualize myself free of debt—writing the check to pay the final balance and CELEBRATING!

Basically, I did everything EXCEPT accept the reality of our debt.

As I said, most Law of Attraction techniques do work to an extent, but they require an environment of non-resistance to really make big things move. The truth was my refusal to look at the sum total of our debt created so much resistance that there was absolutely no way for the Divine to push through and help me.

Soon after that day in the cemetery, I called a friend and confided how angry and scared I really felt. She told me she knew people who had accumulated and paid off way more than that and I could too.

The first step was to get all the debt down on paper so I could build a strategy to pay it off. She offered to sit on the phone with me as I did it. She didn't do anything while she was on the phone with me—she just let me be not alone.

Until that moment I hadn't realized how alone I had felt in all this. My husband was still out of work, and every time we started to look at the money issues with me, he got so panicked that it was worse to involve him. He needed to find a job, and I needed his eye on that ball.

So to finally have someone to just be with me created space for me to breathe and start to really look at all of it.

Once I saw how big the number was, I started to consider hard decisions we hadn't made before. Our children were in private school because the school district we lived in wasn't ideal. We also owned our home and had two new-ish cars.

I started to let in the idea that maybe we would just have to accept our kids needed to go to public school, or we'd have to downsize or give up a car. Previously, I'd considered these choices to be the opposite of positive thinking. In fact, being without these things—private school, cars, etc.—used to make me feel like I had failed, so I avoided thinking about it. If I did think about it, I thought I was somehow lowering my vibration.

But the opposite was true. Not allowing in the actual reality of our debt—and choices we had to make—kept all the solutions out.

But when we started to consider these possibilities, we shifted our thinking, and that opened things up for us. Ultimately, we never had to make any of those tough decisions.

A few months after I started this journey, a serendipitous conversation with a family member led me to confide how stressed I was with our debt. I never would have been able to admit that to her had I not already acknowledged my fear and anger and accepted the size of our debt.

She told me she could lend me money to help us. I was shocked. It never occurred to me to ask a family member for financial help. This just wasn't something we did. But that loan ultimately allowed us to exit the trap that the recurring interest of credit cards had put us in.

There are other miracles that happened along the path— unexpected sums of money showing up along the way, my business growing in ways I hadn't expected, and Matt receiving an amazing job offer out of the blue—that helped us finally get out from underneath that crushing debt.

And we were able to do it without putting our kids in a school we would have worried about or downsizing our home.

But only when we accepted that this might be our truth were we able to truly accept our reality, and only then could the journey of miracles and magic happen.

I'm intentionally leaving out the parts of this story where money magically showed up because I don't want you to cling to those being your answer. Answers will come, but figuring out what you are resisting is the key to finding those answers.

Receiving the External Good Stuff

Big, scary debt is one example of something you might be resisting, but it can be something much smaller as well. In The Receiving School®, one of the first assignments each person takes is to "receive everything." This means if someone gives you a compliment or money or an offer of a gift, you accept it.

Seems simple right? Wrong!

As hard as it was to look at my debt number, it was even more excruciating to accept that help from family. And I find when people start to "receive everything," they are shocked to learn how much good stuff they push away ordinarily.

Sarah desperately needed a break. As a mother of two young children and a caretaker for her aging parents (one with dementia), she was ready to break. Her husband regularly worked overtime to make money to cover their bills, and because he worked so hard, she felt bad asking his help when he got home late after a sixteen-hour workday.

She mentioned this to a friend, who invited her to a three-day trip to her timeshare on the beach and even offered to pay her airfare.

Sarah confided in our community chat room that she was really struggling with saying yes to this generous offer. Of course the community rallied around and reminded her that she needed to get away—she was ready to break.

She told me that, had she not committed to the rule of "receive everything," she wouldn't have even been able to *consider* saying yes.

Ultimately, she did say yes, and amazing things happened. Her husband refused extra work so he could be at home with the kids while she was away—something *she* desperately needed! Her sister-in-law flew in to help her husband so he could also have some downtime. And when she returned, she felt alive again for the first time. That numbness she had started to see as her "normal" faded.

The biggest challenge in receiving gifts like time, money, and support—even when we both want and need them—is that deep down we feel that receiving is selfish. And underneath that fear that we are selfish is the fear that we may be rejected if we are deemed selfish.

The wonderful news is as we allow these gifts in, despite our feelings that we may be deemed selfish, we start to see that not only are we safe and loved, but our relationships grow even stronger.

If you are eager to play with Rule #1, receiving your outer world, visit www.PattyLennon.com/MSFMresources to access 5 simple strategies to get your receiving muscle working!

Chapter 12
Rule #2:
Receive Yourself

One of the big hurdles I had to overcome when releasing our debt was to let go of the belief that I, Patty, was a certain way. Before we got into debt, I always had money—lots of money. So I had a firm belief that "Patty" was a person that always had plenty of money. She would not need money. If anything, she was the one who lent it to others.

This belief extended past money into many areas of my life. The belief was that I wasn't (couldn't be) the "needy" one. I was the one that gave.

If I had been able to accept this "needy" part of myself early on in the process, I don't believe the debt (or my exhaustion levels) would have gotten to the frightening levels that they did. I would have asked for help early on.

But I walked my journey as I did and learned much along the way. My hope is that the struggles I faced can be transformed into teaching that will make your path easier.

As people engage the Five Rules of Receiving, receiving themselves seems to be the piece that makes the biggest overall impact on people's lives.

This may sound counterintuitive to what you believe. Most people come into this process believing the shift in the external circumstances is what will change their experience of life.

They believe they'll be happier if their money issues are resolved, or if they find a loving partner or someone to support them. They understand there must be something "inside" that needs to shift to make this outer reality change, but they believe the outer reality changing is what will give them peace, joy, and love.

I get it. That day in the cemetery, I most certainly believed I could not experience deep peace until my debt was gone. Yet I did. That peace comes from being at peace with myself. And that is what our other members find as well.

When Laura, an amazing artist, joined The Receiving School®, she said she mainly wanted to bring in more money. Like most people, she knew she had trouble receiving. She was always taking care of others, and this idea that "receiving" might be the thing to shift appealed to her.

Then, a few weeks in, she heard me tell someone else, "One day, you will wake up and you will feel deeply in love with yourself." She said that moment a light went on for her, and she knew that was what she really wanted.

One of the tools we provide to help our clients connect to the "rejected self" that most wants to be received and re-integrated is a guided meditation. When Laura did this meditation she connected with her brave and courageous self, someone who was bold and took risks—just the opposite of Laura's day-to-day persona.

When you reject parts of yourself, you not only have trouble receiving, but you also reject the part of yourself that often has the answer to your greatest challenges.

We reject parts of ourselves that feel "negative." But the "negative" is really just the shadow expression of a really beautiful aspect of our personality. As a child, Laura had been taught that being quiet and accommodating was a good thing. Good people didn't show off, and they didn't color outside the lines.

Hence she believed this part of her was bad, and she locked it away. But that brave and courageous part was the part that knew how to self-express. It was the part that saw color and life in new ways and wanted to throw them up on a canvas and show them to the world! The brave and courageous part didn't need to do what was safe—she needed to do what was right for her and feel life in all things!

As a painter, Laura had been painting landscapes, yet her soul was calling her toward abstract work. It felt like landscapes were safe and more sellable, so that's why she had focused on them. But through this work, she let herself see herself accurately. She was an abstract painter!

As she boldly offered this work to the world, something magical started to happen. She started winning awards and prizes for her work. It got to the point where she said she actually felt guilty applying for any award because she knew she'd get it—it almost didn't seem fair.

But even with all her artistic success, she says the real gift is that something she didn't think was possible happened—she fell in love with herself.

It is hard to understand the impact our rejected selves have on our sense of wellbeing. The resistance we hold to just keep those parts away keeps so many external gifts away (like fame, money, and the love of others), but the real tragedy in rejecting ourselves is that we keep us away from ourselves.

Once we start to receive those parts back, we start to feel whole—and that wholeness is the foundation of peace.

Receive Yourself

It would be impossible to do the deep work we do in The Receiving School® in a book like this, but I can tell you a simple place to start.

Although there are so many parts of ourselves that we might reject, I find that for 90 percent of people, there are three parts that we are taught to reject:

1. Needy self
2. Lazy self
3. Selfish self

Regardless of your family of origin or background, the consensus in our society is that being needy, lazy, or a selfish is objectively a "bad" thing.

This couldn't be further from the truth. Each of these words simply describes the "shadow" or negative experience of important human traits. Every part has a shadow and a light side. When you reject a part of yourself, it is usually because you have avoided a particular trait at such an extreme level that you lose connection to the positive aspect of that trait.

No one wants to be rejected. So when we learn that certain traits will potentially get us kicked out of the "tribe," we learn to modify our personal identity to remove all risk of being identified with a "negative" trait.

The light side of "needy" would be the ability to ask for help in a healthy way. The light side of "lazy" would be the ability to honor the need for rest and relaxation. The light side of "selfish" is the ability to honor what is right for us.

These are good qualities! How do we come to label them so negatively? Many times we learn behaviors are unacceptable indirectly as children, when our brains haven't developed the complex structure that can differentiate between being needy and asking for help.

In my case, I learned early on that being "needy" was not okay. It wasn't because my parents ever told me not to be needy; it was because many other people in my parents' lives were already so needy. As I watched my parents—especially my mom—try to help these needy people, I could feel she was close to her breaking point. And I perceived that ANY need was dangerous. I felt like if too much was added to her plate, the whole plate might topple, and that felt incredibly scary to me.

I learned how to need as little as possible—and I was rewarded for it. I got all As in school. I learned to take care of as much around the house as possible. I swallowed any need unless I was desperate.

The adults rewarded me with praise and words of affirmation. Having all the people around me tell me I was "good" because I didn't need anything was what taught me that the opposite must be true—that having needs was bad.

And so I shoved the part of me that had needs far, far away.

The problem with rejecting the shadow side of "needy" is that I also locked away the light side of that personality trait—the ability to ask for help.

How hard is it for you to ask for help—especially when you don't absolutely need it? If you answered, "Ugh, SO HARD!" I want you to ask yourself this question:

How would you feel if someone you cared about told you that you were "needy"?

The Upside of Being Needy

If just thinking about that question makes your stomach turn or face flame with embarrassment, I can promise you that you are rejecting your "needy" self—and this rejection is what has locked away the part of you that can ask for help in a healthy way.

On top of that, the part of you that has needs exists. In order to keep her locked away, you use a LOT of resistance. And that resistance strengthens the field of resistance around you, which keeps all blessings just outside your door.

If you have been visualizing , staying positive, and feeling "as if" for years and have not experienced manifestation that matches your manifesting effort, most likely the resistance of your self-rejection is also keeping the blessings away.

Before I started to receive this "needy" part of myself, I often felt lonely. I had become so good at not needing anything EVER that very few people offered to help me—even my husband.

I lived the story that "I do not need (help, support, etc.)," and I got so good at weaving that story that even the man I was the most vulnerable with—the one who saw me at my lowest points—still believed I didn't need anything.

It was my mom's journey through cancer that let me first glimpse this toxic independence that had been passed down through the women in my family. But it wasn't until my dad died that I truly let the needy part of myself fully integrate into my conscious life.

I just didn't have anything to give, and I knew enough not to keep trying to summon up energy from an empty well. I was grieving. End of story. As I made this part of myself more known, miraculous things started to happen.

My kids helped more. My husband started to see all the holes in our domestic balance. He wanted to help, and suddenly the places he could help became obvious.

Simple things—like making our bed in the morning—became a ritual for him, a way of caring for me when my heart was so broken. The thing is, we had been married for eighteen years at that point. How was it that making the bed suddenly became visible to him? In the past I would have said he needed to change. He needed to see all that I was doing and choose to help. But the truth is he didn't change. He has always wanted the best for me, always wanted to show me love. *I* changed. My inner shift at needing to be cared for created the space for him to see what I needed.

By the end of that year that my dad died, I felt more whole and less lonely. Even in the midst of "losing" my last parent, I felt less alone. My grief had created a safe space for my needy self to return, and blessings flowed.

Much has changed in the balance in our home since then. I can't say it's all because of accepting this "needy" part of myself, but it's definitely in large part because of it. My husband and I have talked often about it.

He describes it as if suddenly it was so obvious how much weight I was carrying. He said he truly didn't see it before. He's also explained that it is very hard to help me sometimes because I always seem so confident. It feels like he's more in the way than helpful.

As I was writing this chapter in the book, I was wondering whether this was a dynamic in our marriage or if others truly felt this way as well. And coincidentally, we ended up going out to dinner with our friends, Steph and John.

They were reflecting on the success of a recent training I had given where two thousand people had participated in learning The Receiving Method. John was talking about how crazy it was that I had felt so lost at one point on this journey—and look at where I was now!

Steph was talking about how unsure I was about how everything would unfold.

I laughed and said, "Well yeah—I was giving up a business I knew made money and stepping onto a path I had no idea about. Of course I was unsure!"

And then Steph said something that shocked me. "It's not normal for you, Patty. In the entire time I've known you, that is the only time I've ever seen you question anything. You always seem confident. You always seem to know what to do next."

I pushed back. Steph has seen me at some pretty low points. How could she think I always know what to do? But John continued, "No, Patty. You ALWAYS seem confident."

And then my husband chimed in. "Patty, I've told you this. You never seem to doubt where you are headed. You always seem to know the next best step."

I was floored. These three people had witnessed me at some pretty deep lows, and yet none of them had perceived my doubt and fear except at that point in my life where I let my needy self fully express herself.

When I thought I was "needy," others simply saw me as human—vulnerable and in doubt.

When we reject parts of ourselves, we often hold a skewed perception of that quality. Because I was working so hard to reject the needy part of myself, anytime the faintest whiff of need bubbled up to me, it felt really big—like I was walking around the world as a sniveling need-ball.

But to the people around me, they perceived this faint whiff of need as a challenge that I already had under control.

This skewed reality we experience often leads us to set ourselves up to go without what we most need.

In the past, I had often thought, "Why isn't anybody helping me? Can't they see I'm struggling?" And the answer was that no, they could not see my struggle.

When we start to accept these parts of ourselves that we rejected, we can have a more normalized reaction to situations, reactions that others can perceive. As I reintegrated this "needy" self, others could respond to those needs.

Right now, if you feel run down or like you are always carrying more of the weight on your shoulders and wonder why you always have to ask to get any kind of help, there is a good chance that you also are rejecting your needy self.

Here is what I want you to understand: everyone around you isn't selfish and taking you for granted. Maybe that's true for some people, but more likely, the people around you can't see where you need help. You have a thick, energetic cloak up around your needs because you are working so hard to keep your "needy" self packed away.

What would happen if you let yourself feel needy? That answer has the power to release resistance right now.

The "Selfish" Self

The rejection of the "selfish" self is closely related to this needy self. When we reject the "selfish" self, we have decided that honoring what we need is bad. Or maybe you just tell yourself, "When everyone else around me is happy and taken care of, then I can worry about myself."

Starting to integrate the "selfish" self can be one of the most challenging integrations, because if you have rejected this part, you most likely have also learned to wear the label "selfless" like a badge of honor. This is especially true in care-takers, whether you have children or are caring for an aging parent or someone ill.

Your initial desire to put another person's needs was likely an authentic one. But we aren't meant to put our needs aside for years and certainly not a lifetime. At some point suppressing your own needs will create restlessness and even resentment. It is hard to pinpoint where this is coming from, and as you attempt to "solve" the problem, you'll feel a bit lost.

This is because the answer you are looking for that will free you from restlessness and resentment is locked away. What you need has been labeled "selfish" by you. And you don't want to be "selfish," so you won't allow the answers within you to rise to consciousness.

This happened for my client Megan. She was unfulfilled in her career as a part-time communication consultant. She felt she had a bigger purpose in the world and wasn't using her gifts fully.

When we started working together, Megan knew she needed a change, she just couldn't figure out what that would look like and how to make it happen. What we discovered as we dug in is that Megan had put a lot of rules in place to what she could and could not do. And those rules tied back to not wanting to be selfish.

Those rules had trapped her in her current career. She also found those rules also extended far beyond the work she did. As we started to explore what Megan would choose if she trusted the desires inside her, new truths emerged.

Megan started to see that she had blocked out pieces of herself when she became a mother. When her children were babies she chose to leave her career as a well-paid director of community relations to be with them full time. She made this choice out of love—she didn't do it because she had to and it certainly wasn't meant to be permanent.

But as her children grew, she lost track of her original motivation and slipped into an identity of "good mom." That identity was defined by society more than herself. An identity which told her she shouldn't want a high-powered career and salary to match it if it meant she wasn't there for her children when they got home (even if they were well into their teen years).

"It feels selfish taking a full-time job when they might need me."

That one comment unlocked a world of limitations Megan had put on herself. She felt she had so much to be grateful for;

who was she to want so much more? And yet, we discovered, she did. It turns out, for example, that despite being a "good mom" she didn't want to have to make family meals any longer. (I assured her very few of us did.)

As we pulled back the layers of all the choices Megan was making today that left her feeling tired, overwhelmed, or just plain uninspired, it always came back to one concern—if she made a different choice, she'd be selfish.

There is nothing wrong with putting off goals and dreams if you do so consciously. There are many reasons that can lead a person to say, "I want this, just not right now." But when we refuse to acknowledge what we truly want because somehow we are wrong for wanting it, that is what leads us to feel bored, uninspired, and even worse: angry and resentful.

Megan took on a challenge to make small shifts that her mind told her were selfish but her heart told her were necessary. She carved out a new workspace for herself. She began to hand off some meal planning to her teen children and even planned a trip for herself.

As she started to do this, something miraculous happened. She reconnected with an earlier version of herself. She was able to remember who she was at twenty when everything felt possible. As that connection grew so did her sense of hope and inspiration.

She has decided she still needs a year or two to start pursuing a full-time job, but now that she accepts this, she feels much more free. She's also aware of how much happier she is when she allows herself to honor her dreams and desires. And the best part is the frustration and resentment she was feeling is draining out of her life.

She thought she'd need massive external shifts to make that happen. As it turns out, the shifts she really needed to make were within.

To begin this journey what you need to understand is that honoring yourself and your own needs, no matter how it is labeled, is a good thing. It releases you from feeling trapped by your circumstances. It opens up feelings of health and vitality in you and allows you to feel fully alive.

Megan's family supported her in her changes, but that doesn't always happen. I want to assure you if you follow Megan's lead and don't get the support you need at first, keep going. It's likely the people around you like how "selfless" you are. When you start to take care of your own needs, others who benefited from your "selflessness" may resist your changes.

During these times, it's important to know that the reaction from outside yourself is really a mirror of your fears that you'll be rejected if you take care of yourself. As you gain confidence and integrate this healthy trait, magic does happen. The people who truly love you will appreciate the changes you are making because they are right for YOU!

The "Lazy" Self

The most exhilarating integration is probably that of the "lazy" self. It is also the integration that has the greatest benefit to the world at large. Here is why: when you learn to integrate the "lazy" self, you stop questioning your need to rest.

You are able to listen to what your body needs and follow that guidance. When you do that, your need for unhealthy stimuli (like overdrinking and overeating) starts to dissipate. You are able to honor your mind's need to rest, which in turn improves your mental functioning and makes you better able to see the solutions before you.

This is exactly what happened to my client Lou. Lou had a successful video production and consulting business. He, like many people, equated a good "work ethic" to working all the time. When he came to me, he said he was burnt out.

I suggested he do what I ask most clients to do that feel burnt out—take a vacation. He pushed back. His client flow had slowed tremendously because the pandemic had just started. He felt he had to work even harder because none of us could predict what the pandemic would mean.

I explained that the vacation I was recommending would actually bring clients in. This vacation wasn't about visiting some tropical destination; in fact, he didn't even need to leave home. It was about disconnecting from obligation and agenda so he could refill his well.

I have been giving this homework assignment for years so I have confidence in its ability to shift things for anyone in any circumstance, but I knew I had to translate it into terms Lou could understand. I told him that clients feel our vibration (which is completely true). They hire us because of how we make them feel—and right then people could feel his depletion. As he refilled his well, clients would respond.

In truth, this works because as we stop *doing* and allow ourselves to rest and recharge, we release tremendous resistance. As this resistance drops away, it is easier for the Universe to deliver what we most desire to us with ease.

Lou was dubious, but he said he trusted me so was willing to give it a try. He booked a stay at a cabin in the woods, disconnected from technology, and rested. A few weeks after his return, a big business opportunity landed on his doorstep. Even though the pandemic conditions slowed many businesses down, Lou had one of his best years.

Lou, a self-proclaimed cynic, now calls me his "spiritual consigliere." I have to admit, it is one of my favorite titles. To become someone's trusted spiritual advisor is a privilege I don't take lightly. Integrating these rejected selves is spiritual work.

The Divine does not want you to feel that you must always be *doing* to have what you desire. In fact, She loves you so much it makes Her happy to see you slow down and enjoy life.

Most people I know reject their "lazy" self. If you suspect you are doing the same and feel exhausted, uninspired, or just plain burnt out, take some time to rest. Yes, it may feel lazy, but it is good—I promise you!

As you do all this, you start to show others how to do the same for themselves. We are living and raising our children in a culture of exhaustion. There is absolutely no way we can ever get to the heights of nonviolence, equity, and balance that so many of us want if we don't learn to shake off the fog of fatigue.

Learning how to discover and reintegrate our rejected selves isn't a straightforward process. It's a delicate balance of integration and honoring the fear and trauma that caused you to reject parts of yourself to begin with.

There are many parts of ourselves that we can pack away, but if any part of my "needy" story resonated with you, here is where I suggest you start.

Ask yourself, "If I knew it was a good thing to be needy, what would I do differently?" That answer will take you on a journey of self-discovery that will open up worlds of possibility.

If you see yourself in Megan's or Lou's stories, start there.

This is deep work, and it can be difficult to do on your own. If you want to explore this further, I'd love to have you join us in The Receiving School® here: www.thereceivingschool.com.

Chapter 13

Rule #3:
Clear Space to Make Space

Receiving rejected parts of ourselves is BIG work, and it often happens slowly over time. I have found this work can be frustrating at times because it is slow. Which is why Rule #3—Clear Space to Make Space—is often a breath of fresh air in the midst of doing this work.

When I say "clear space," I'm talking about literally clearing your physical space.

Every object, every piece of matter, is made of energy and so holds energy. That energy can be good for us—or it can block us.

When we look at a beautiful picture in our home or fresh flowers and feel like we can breathe more deeply—that we have more space inside of us—those objects are opening us to receiving.

But the reverse is also true. When we have a corner of a room filled with junk—or even a pile of papers we haven't dealt with yet and are filled with a heaviness or sense of dread—those objects are creating resistance for us.

A lot of this work we've already covered can feel intangible, but our stuff is most definitely tangible, making it a great place to focus when you want to have a simple, straightforward process to open you up to receiving.

Clearing Clutter

After my dad passed away, I was named the executrix of his estate. This meant that I needed to take care of all the paperwork associated with his affairs. Every day it felt like more and more paper arrived.

In the first weeks after he passed, I didn't have the bandwidth to really process all the paperwork that was coming through, so I'd open it, see if it required immediate attention, and if it didn't, add it to a growing pile of paperwork on my dining room table.

I had a long dining room table, so there was plenty of space for the paperwork and my family of four to eat. But it meant that every meal we shared together also included the weight of the responsibility of closing out my dad's estate.

At first, I was numb, so allowing that paperwork to just sit there was a loving gift I gave myself. In the past, my control-freak self would have been constantly addressing each piece of paper that arrived as it arrived.

Eventually, though, this pile of paper just felt like a constant reminder that my dad wasn't there and that I had a lot of work to do to let him go.

Finally, I prayed for guidance on how to move through the next months of estate work without feeling like a heavy burden was constantly on my shoulders. Almost immediately, I had the inspiration to buy a portable file container.

I stopped what I was doing—sensing a bit of freedom for the first time where this was concerned—rushed out to Target, and bought a giant bin and file folders.

It took me an entire weekend, but I got all the papers organized and filed and stored in our closet. Once I did, I realized the actual amount of work I had to do was much less than I had imagined. I also let go of the sense that it all needed to happen right now, which gave me much more space to breathe.

That is the value of clearing our clutter.

Clearing clutter also gives us a tangible way to work with what is stuck inside us. For me, trying to ignore that paperwork kept me in a place somewhere between having my dad and letting him go.

As I sorted through that paperwork, I shed *a lot* of tears. Simple things—like his electric bill—reminded me of how he liked to stay up late at night reading by the light of a single lamp.

Each seemingly insignificant document helped me face the loss I was avoiding feeling.

It's easy to think clutter is just clutter, but almost always clutter is something we are avoiding looking at. Once we start to sort through, we find spaciousness and release in places we were scared to look.

That happened to one of my clients, Susan. We were working through the "clearing space" part of our coursework when she found herself stuck in clearing out a hallway.

She told me she felt silly being unable to clear the stuff cluttering up her hallway because it was getting on her nerves. Why couldn't she just get rid of what was there?

I had her walk me slowly through what was there. A big part of the "junk" in her hallway was sports equipment belonging to her daughter.

I asked her, "Can you turn this responsibility over to your daughter?"

She responded that she could, but most of it didn't even fit her anymore.

So then I pressed further—"Well, does she want to keep it for sentimental reasons? Can your daughter move it to her room?"

Just then Susan's eyes filled with tears. She was laughing and crying at the same time. She told me her daughter had no attachment to the items and donating them had already been discussed.

She just now was realizing that if she was to let all this go, she'd have to accept her daughter was done with high school sports. Her daughter was preparing to go to college, and getting rid of this sports equipment would require Susan to accept her daughter was moving on.

All this time, she thought she was stuck with this clutter, but what she was stuck in was resisting the truth her little girl was growing up.

She gave herself some time to release the items in her hallway, but what gave her immediate relief was to understand what all this junk really was—proof of how much she loved her little girl.

Release What Doesn't Serve

Letting go of things that once had value for us can be hard—especially when there is sentimental value in those things.

The thought I use to help myself release what no longer serves me is to remember that every object was created with a highest purpose. A fork, a shoe, a painting—everything has its own energy and the ability to manifest its highest purpose if we let it.

When we hold on to things that no longer serve us, we keep those objects from helping others.

Sports equipment that is donated can then be used for a younger athlete who needs it, and giving it away allows the mitt or the ball to continue to operate at its highest level.

This is also true of objects that we don't like and have no value. These are often hardest to release because the reason we keep them is out of fear.

As I walk clients through this "clearing space" training, what is hardest to release are the items that stick around out of fear, guilt, obligation, or the thought that "I might need that someday."

It's always fascinating to me that something we don't like can be so hard to release.

Jackie, a client of mine, had a large brass vase that sat on her mantel above her fire. She told me she despised it. Every time she looked at it, it made her a little bit angry.

"So why not release it?" I asked.

"My mother-in-law gave it to use on our wedding day, and I feel like my husband would be hurt if I tried to get rid of it."

I suggested she ask him that night if he would mind getting rid of it, considering it was such a point of resistance for her. He admitted he didn't like it much either and gave her free rein to dispose of or donate it.

The next time we spoke, I asked her how it felt being free from the angry brass vase. Jackie told me with some embarrassment that she didn't feel that different. When I explored why that was, she admitted that she hadn't completely gotten rid of it. She just moved it to her closet.

She was afraid to donate it because her mother-in-law might notice the next time she visited. Even though the vase was off her mantel, she could still "feel" it in the house.

As we slowly unwound the story of why Jackie was really holding onto the vase, what she discovered is that she always felt her mother-in-law's presence around them, even though she rarely visited.

Her mother-in-law was a tough woman who had spent most of her life cooking and cleaning and having very little pleasure in her own life. Anytime Jackie made life easy on herself, she had a vague sense that she wasn't measuring up to what her husband expected or what her mother-in-law would have done in her place.

Once she saw what was really keeping her from receiving the ease she so desperately wanted, she confided in her husband what was going on. He loved her and was frustrated that she did always seem to make life so hard on herself. When he started to understand what she thought he expected from her, he was able to support her in creating more ease for herself.

He told her the last thing he wanted was for another woman he loved to always work so hard and never find the joy that he felt both she and his mother deserved.

The next day, Jackie dropped the vase at her local donation center and left with a new sense of freedom.

All this amazing truth came from clearing one brass vase from a fireplace mantel!

Chapter 14

Rule #4:
Learn Your Language

When you begin the journey of receiving the world around you and then receiving yourself, you may feel afraid, lost, or alone at first. Don't worry; this will pass. These feelings arise simply because our brain is trying to make sense of a new reality.

It is easy to want to reach for some of the people around you to witness and "approve" of your journey.

Resist that urge, because they may not have the courage to join you, and their urge to keep you from changing will be to keep you stuck.

But you are not alone. There are Beings who can support you—the Divine, your Spirit Guides, loved ones, and angels— all ready to jump in and give you the comfort, encouragement, and love you desire. They have massive amounts of love and support and guidance to give you because they see and honor your path.

In order to tap into that support and guidance, you must learn how they communicate with you and how you can communicate back to them. Essentially, you need to learn a new language. A language of visions, inspirations, signs, and metaphysical directives.

The good news is that this language is part of a Universal order that already exists in the world. At first you may wonder if you are getting the messages correct, but eventually you'll learn to trust it.

Because of the way the media has portrayed metaphysical communication, most of us grow up thinking that communicating with the other side of the veil is only possible for some people. And those people already know who they are. Those people were able to "know things" from a young age and talk to dead people. Those people have visions of future events and predictive abilities.

What I find is that most people have a narrow understanding of how to communicate with the other side of the veil. They believe that they must be clairvoyant to communicate with their spiritual support team.

Clairvoyance is the psychic gift of sight. This means you see things you wouldn't normally be able to see with your human eyes.

The truth is that only a small portion of our population possesses the gift of clairvoyance, but everyone has gifts. Understanding how those gifts show up helps us tap into our unique language.

Have you ever sensed that you have intuitive gifts you aren't using?

Or maybe you'd just like to understand better how to develop your intuitive gifts so that when you are receiving information, you know how to use it.

Everyone has intuitive gifts—the key is learning how to tap into them.

Unlike most people who teach about intuition and taking intuitive gifts deeper, I wasn't always able to access my own gifts. In fact, I spent most of my life living as what Harry Potter fans would call "a muggle."

I am a former type-A corporate banker who suddenly found myself at the age of thirty-seven "knowing" things I had never previously known. Over the last fifteen years, I've learned to cultivate those gifts, so I can tell you with certainty that having previous access to gifts is no predictor of how successful you will be using them in the future. Learning to tap your intuitive gifts is about learning your language.

Toward the end of my banking career, I began a coaching certification program with Martha Beck, a well-known coach and teacher. By then I had committed to leaving banking and launching my own coaching business focused on helping others create the life they desired.

As part of the program, I attended a retreat with Martha in the desert. She was easy to learn from because although she had metaphysical leanings, she also held a PhD from Harvard, and her traditional credentials appealed to my pragmatic mind.

During our time together I started to know and feel things about the other attendees. Things I had no reason to know. I shared the information coming through to me with those attendees—and over the course of those few days, each one confirmed the information I was receiving was correct.

From that point on, my intuitive gifts grew incrementally. I'm still not clear why my gifts opened at that particular moment. It's possible that leaving the security of banking and having faith in where I was being guided unlocked that magic.

It's also possible that the combination of teacher, place, and community created enough safety for my mind to finally release its resistance to the gifts that lay dormant. Or more likely a combination of all these things.

I asked my Spirit Guides once why so many intuitive people have stories of having gifts as a young child—when I never did.

As I said, I was quite muggly my whole early life. They told me this was something I specifically chose so that I'd know exactly what it felt like to walk around the world without access to the information that is available to every single one of us.

My early life "blocks" were there precisely so I could show you how to unblock your own gifts and help you learn YOUR language.

What I've found is most helpful to understand is that there are many different kinds of intuitive gifts, but media has led us to believe that one or two of them are more "real" than others.

I used to think if someone really had "gifts," they'd be able to hear and see all kinds of freaky stuff. That isn't how it works for most people; generally speaking, intuitive gifts are subtle.

The Clairs

That being said, let me explain the five types of intuitive gifts that are the most common so you can identify the gifts you likely have and may already be using right now.

Clairvoyance is the gift of sight, the ability to see things. This is the gift most media build a lot of hype around. You've probably seen some movie or read a book where the intuitive sees a crash before it happens or touches an object and the person that owns that object is brought to life right before their eyes.

Although clairvoyance is a very cool gift, it is not the gift I find most people access first (if at all). But so often, when I am helping people lean into their own gifts to access guidance, they expect that they should be able to "see" something. This just isn't the case.

The second gift is *clairaudience*, the ability to hear something. This is also a gift the media likes to focus on. Clairvoyance and clairaudience are easy to portray in the media, and this is why writers and directors lean so heavily on them.

The most common gifts I've encountered in people are not so easy to portray. They are called claircognizance and clairsentience.

Claircognizance occurs when you suddenly know something you have no previous access to. Have you ever known something although you couldn't explain how you knew it? If so, it is likely that this is the seat of your "language." This is how the other side speaks to you.

Clairsentience happens when you can feel information. This, I find, is the most "normal" channel of communication for those of us who are sensitive. Do you feel or sense things without knowing how that happens? If that is you, then it is likely that the Divine, your loved one, and Spirit Guides will use this "emotional pathway" to speak to you and offer you guidance, and clairsentience is your gift. For me, when I started to understand that what I was feeling was communication, it helped me find guidance much more quickly.

The thing about all these forms of communication is that they are subtle. They speak in whispers, so our work initially is to quiet ourselves down and not always be busy.

Meditation is a beautiful way to get to this "quiet space," but even if meditation isn't your thing, creating space away from technology, other people, and sounds will help you start to connect to the subtle language you are receiving.

Taking walks in nature or simply sitting by a tree or running water can be so valuable in helping you open up to the gentle whispers your soul is receiving. The more you notice, the more you'll be able to receive this communication.

Once you start building your "receiving muscle," you'll find that it is easier to receive guidance and that you are more able to tap the flow that is inherent in the Universe. The more you lean into the flow, the easier life gets.

But that flow can be counterintuitive. It can guide us to the left when we know our destination is to the right. It can ask us to stop and rest when we are eager to finish.

As you allow yourself to receive, knowing where the flow of life is asking you to go becomes obvious. Finding the courage to follow it is another story.

When the guidance is asking something that feels scary or hard, there is another "language" that I find is really helpful. That is the language of *signs*.

The Language of Signs

Signs are helpful because they are "real"—or at least they feel more concrete.

That was the place I was in after my mom died.

Having witnessed her struggle to receive any type of support, I started to wake up to my own resistance in that area. I wasn't the receiving machine I am today, but I was making progress. And that progress allowed me to tap into this flow in a deeper way.

Every day the Divine's whisper, "Trust me," grew louder. I was getting messages from my Spirit Guides and also my mom. This mixed and mingled with the deep grief I could feel in every cell. I was learning to adjust to a world where my mom was no longer physically here but was leaving me messages that she was close.

About a month after she passed, I felt the push from her and my Spirit Guides to start to live with the truth that she was not coming back. One of the things I could "feel" I had to do was erase the last voice message I had from her. I played it over and over again, and I could see it was keeping me trapped in the past—in a place where she had a human voice, a human touch.

If I was going to move forward, I had to let go of wanting that experience back and connect more fully to the place she was in now.

I asked for help doing this, and what I was guided to do was to take a personal retreat. I found a retreat center an hour away and decided to give myself a day to just be with whatever came up. At the end of that day, I would delete her message.

I also committed to follow flow, no matter what. I had no idea how I was going to go from the place I was in emotionally to a place where I could hit delete on that message, and yet I felt that Divine whisper, "Trust me, trust me." And so I did.

As I pulled out of my driveway, I was guided to a road that would not take me directly to the retreat center. Every brain cell said to turn in the opposite direction, but following my commitment to follow flow, I went where flow led me.

I ended up in front of Yale New Haven Hospital. This was the place my mom had received many treatments along her path with cancer. As I sat there, I wondered why I was brought there.

Was I supposed to go in? See where so much had happened? Thank the staff? What? What? What? My mind grasped for answers—for reasons.

That grasping is one of the ways our mind can get in the way of hearing the language of the Divine and our other metaphysical helpers. The other side of the veil speaks in whispers, while our mind directs us in shouts.

I sat there in my car, idling outside the hospital, wondering if I would get my answer before a traffic officer asked me to move. I began to breathe, intentionally filling my lungs, holding my breath for four counts and releasing it—the only type of breathing I had found could calm my mind.

Breathe in, hold, breathe out.

As my nervous system slowed, I could feel the distant thrum of a whisper. It was almost as if I knew it was speaking, but my mind hadn't quieted quite enough to hear its instructions.

Suddenly I felt a body of wisdom—the Divine? my Guides?—guiding me to pull myself back from inside the hospital. I didn't even understand what that meant at first, and then I felt it.

I had left parts of myself inside the hospital. With each treatment, each hour that passed waiting for answers, for hope, I had left pieces of myself.

I started to call them back. I felt them enter my body. When I described the process to a healer months later, she told me it sounds like I had been guided in a soul retrieval. I'm still not sure whether that was the case, but by the end of the day, I did feel steadier in the world. That was the first stop in my journey.

Following this guidance with faith can be challenging for my clients (and for me). Sometimes it feels like inner guidance is playing us for a fool.

As I sat there in front of the hospital, I had one of those moments. I thought I had just done a momentous thing—driving to this hospital, sitting there, sucking in parts of my left-behind soul. Yay me. But no—I wasn't finished.

I felt my attention pulled across the street to a farmer's market. The whisper said, "Go there!"

It was raining. Stand outside in a farmer's market?

Really?

What happened next reminded me that our journey isn't always about us. We are co-creating this world with others, and sometimes guidance is for them.

I halfheartedly tried to negotiate with the guidance, but I've learned guidance rarely comes with options. We can choose to ignore it, but we can't change it.

So I parked my car, walked to the farmer's market, and stood in the rain. A flower stand caught my eye.

I had to buy flowers (guidance instructed).

Really? Flowers? The flowers were going to be sitting in the car for six hours. It made no sense. I followed the guidance anyway.

I picked out a bunch of gerbera daisies. "Do you have any paper towels I could wrap them in? They're going to be sitting in the car for a while," I asked the man with the flowers.

The flower man did me one better. With much care, he wrapped the flowers in ice and newspaper. "I'm not very good at this," he said.

"Are you kidding me? That's the best wrap job I've ever seen!" I laughed.

"You are my first sale today. Thank you so much," he said quietly. He smiled a little. It was then that I read the stand's sign: "Roses for Autism." I felt the zing I get when my Guides want me to pay attention to something.

Miracle #1

That was when it hit me. Standing out in the rain at the farmer's market wasn't about me. It was about him, the flower man. He needed a sale. And I needed to feel a part of something bigger than myself.

I drove off feeling lighter somehow.

I arrived at the retreat center and instantly "knew" the flowers were for someone inside. I picked up the flowers and walked inside, thinking my inner guidance best be right, because I did not want to be dragging those flowers around my retreat all day.

Inside I met Betty of Guest Services. Without thinking, I handed her the flowers.

"Oh! These are for you!" I said, surprised my hand knew that before I did.

I wanted to tell Betty the story of how they had come to arrive in her office, but before I could get the words out, she said, "You have no idea how much this means to me. I needed this today of all days."

The warm glow of being part of something bigger than myself filled me up again. (Note to self: Stop questioning inner guidance—inner guidance rocks!)

Betty pointed me in the direction I wanted to go and gave me a hug, and I headed off.

A few minutes later I heard my name. I turned around to see Betty coming to me.

"Please wait. I'm not sure I can say this without crying." (She was already crying.) "I didn't see this when you handed me the flowers." She pointed to the "Roses for Autism" label. "My two grandchildren are autistic. I couldn't possibly tell you what this means to me. These really are for me!"

Miracle #2

And there it was—the *real* reason I needed to stand out in the rain at a farmer's market. I was a channel of faith for Betty, and I was being given an extra shot of faith for a difficult day. But the miracles didn't stop there . . .

Later that day, I deleted the last message my mom left me before she died.

It was hard, so very hard, but I did it.

It wasn't until Monday that I discovered the third miracle the farmer's market had brought me.

I received an email from Betty, thanking me for the flowers and telling me once again what they had meant to her. She had been deeply worried about her grandchildren. They were little, but she was scared what their future would hold because of their autism. She loved them and wasn't sure how to help them. She asked for a sign. The next day I arrived with those flowers.

I started to reply that it was my pleasure and that it was exactly the type of thing my mom would have done. And that is when it hit me: My mom would have been the first to deliver flowers to a fellow grandmother struggling with faith. And she would have bought flowers she didn't need from someone simply because that person needed the sale. And she was always there when her children needed her.

Miracle #3

My mom was there.

The morning of the retreat, I had asked my mom to be with me and to give me the courage I needed to delete her message, to let her go. And she used a farmer's market, five daisies, and two miracles to make sure I knew she heard me and that she'd always be there.

Magical occurrences like that happen for me weekly, sometimes daily, now that I've learned to listen to the language the Universe is using to speak to me.

My clients have had the same experiences.

The $250,000 Demand

Take Nell for example. Nell is a successful nonprofit consultant. She originally hired me to grow her business, but as our time together evolved, we found ourselves more focused on developing Nell's intuitive gifts.

As she followed the communication she was getting from the Universe, she found herself guided further and further from actions that in the "real world" would "make her money."

Following this guidance required more and more trust, and I could feel she was starting to get some "trust-fatigue"—a type of exhaustion we feel when our mind is fighting our souls really, REALLY hard.

In one session, her Spirit Guides asked me to ask her what it would take to give up the fight and just trust that they were guiding her properly.

"I don't know. I know this is the direction I should be going in, but it sometimes feels like I'm putting my family at risk. I want proof that the money is going to show up if I keep following this guidance."

Just then, one of her Guides said, "Ask her how much it will take." This made me laugh—like they were ready to pay her mind off to ransom her soul.

I asked Nell, but she waffled. She couldn't quite get to an amount.

"Come on, Nell!" I pushed. "They are giving you a blank check. How much will it take for you to believe?"

Finally, she just blurted out, "$250,000!"

I was stunned. Even though I KNOW money is just energy and the Universe can deliver a dime as easily as a million dollars—it is really hard for us to let in those bigger amounts.

$250,000 felt like a big risk when Nell's trust hinged on it. But just as quickly as those doubts flew through my head, a wave of peace washed over me.

"Done," I heard her Guide say.

I laughed. *Wow, this should be fun.*

A week later I received an email from Nell.

The money hadn't yet arrived, but something had happened. She was reading a book, and words on the page jumped out at her. She said it was like they were glowing.

The passage essentially said that for life to manifest at its highest level there must be trust. Nell felt it was a message from her Guides, urging her to trust so that they could give her the money—her proof.

A few days later, she was working in her office when she heard a sound in another room. She was home alone, so she went to investigate. An ornament had spontaneously fallen off her Christmas tree. When she picked it up, she saw it was an ornament her son had made as a child. It said, "Believe!"

She was laughing now because her Guides were being very persistent. "We'll do this, but you've got to have faith!"

Nell listened.

A few days later she emailed me one of the wildest, amazing-est receiving stories I have ever personally witnessed.

She told me her son had just found out he got into his top college, and he was awarded $240k in scholarships! Not the entire $250k she asked for, but pretty close! And here is the best part:

"I don't know if you remember this, but the whole reason I initially gave for wanting to grow my business and work with you a year ago was because I was terrified of the enormous cost of college we were going to have to incur shortly. So basically, in one night that enormous burden has been completely erased."

Sometimes we think we know what we want for ourselves, but the Universe, the Divine, sees underneath our desires and fulfills our deepest needs. Money was never the issue for Nell, which is why she struggled so much with picking an amount. Knowing her children had options in life, free of debt, was the issue.

She asked for money; the Universe delivered so much more.

The Unique Language of Signs

Do you love to get signs and want to know how to make it happen more often?

I get it. It is very normal to want to get signs. Signs help us feel

- Like the choices we are making are the right choices.
- Like we are supported and most importantly.
- Connected to support from our loved ones, spirit guides, and angels.

No wonder we feel good when we get a sign.

Common Misunderstandings

When I help people learn to ask for and receive signs, I find there are a few misunderstandings that keep many people from actually letting in all the help their "team" from the other side of the veil is sending them.

The first misunderstanding is that signs only come once in a while.

The truth is that you are being given signs all the time—in fact, this book may be a sign. It is very possible that a loved one who has crossed over drew your attention to this book so you could learn how to hear all the messages and signs they are sending you!

The second misunderstanding is that you have to ask for signs in a special way in order to receive them.

Nothing could be further from the truth—your loved ones, angels, and Guides do not need special language or requests to give you support and love.

The third misunderstanding is the belief that "other people" get signs, but you don't. Signs are an equal opportunity level of support that we all receive. If you feel like you aren't getting signs, it's simply because you don't understand the language that is being used.

Let's walk through the three types of signs we all can receive and how to understand their language. I'll also explain who is sending these signs so you can better understand why you are getting them.

Three Types of Signs

General Signs

General signs are universal to all of us—meaning if I saw this sign, it would likely have a similar meaning if you received the sign.

Some very typical general signs are numbers—especially 11:11.

Animals are another general sign. Many people who have a loved one cross over find that they are soon visited by a cardinal—a very typical message of love and connection.

Coins are also a common tool used in signs. There are hundreds of thousands of stories of dimes or pennies from heaven across the internet. I think our loved ones choose these signs simply because there is a common understanding of their meaning.

Personal Signs

Personal signs are specific to you—meaning you are the only person that would receive specific meaning from that particular sign.

Perhaps you and a loved one shared the love of a favorite artist or sports team. It would make sense that they'd have signs and symbols of that shared connection show up to wave at you and say, "Hey, I'm close!"

Chosen Signs

Chosen signs are ones that we ask for specifically. We typically choose signs as a way of proof that a question is being answered. Although I don't use chosen signs very often myself, I find they are very helpful for people who feel doubtful that a sign is a sign.

While it's essential that you understand how the signs may come, you'll also need to shift your perception in order to actually be able to see those signs. As I said, we are all getting signs every day. We are all equally supported, but when you don't see the signs, it's often because your brain is filtering them out.

Reprogram Your Brain to Get Signs

To actually see signs and hear the language of signs, here are the shifts you need to make in your thinking, in the way your brain interacts with the world:

1. Trust your feelings, because signs are based in love. They are communication from a being who loves you and wants you to feel that love and support, so you won't just get a sign—you will feel it. When something feels like a sign, you can trust that it is a sign.

2. Trust synchronicity. If you are thinking of your grandmother who made your favorite chocolate chip cookies, and then you turn on the TV and see a chocolate chip cookie—she's definitely saying hi. Our cynical brain likes to disregard synchronicity, but synchronicity is part of the language of signs.

3. Ask and then open. Although you don't have to ask for a sign to get one, I find most people like asking for signs—especially when they are for specific answers. Once you ask, allow yourself to stay open to getting the sign. Your brain is trained to doubt anything it cannot explain, so when you ask for a sign, it will immediately start to shut down its awareness to that sign coming in. Instead of looking for the answer, simply shift into a "waiting" mode. This means you decide it's coming and it's just a matter of when. Once you decide something, your brain shifts its focus and it stops engaging resistance, allowing the signs to show up far more easily.

There is absolutely nothing you need to do to be worthy of a sign. Signs are a language your loved ones, Guides, and angels use to communicate with you.

If you'd love some help opening to more signs you can find a simple cheat sheet I created, "10 Ways to Get Signs," here: www.PattyLennon.com/MSFMresources

Once you start to notice signs, write them down. I've found that the most powerful way to increase your ability to receive and understand signs is to track them.

This isn't some "woo" theory. This has been proven by strategists and mathematicians dating as far back as the nineteenth century when statistician Karl Pearson created the coefficient of correlation that connected dots in our behavior.

When we track something it improves. When we tell others about what we are tracking it improves exponentially. Keep a journal or note on your phone and jot down a sign when you get it. As you measure signs, the rate at which you receive and understand them will improve.

If you really want to accelerate the growth in becoming fluent in this language, find a place to report what you are seeing. This, to me, is one of the reasons why things shift so quickly for people in The Receiving School® community. Not only are they learning their language, but they are also reporting on what they see and understand, and so fluency is accelerated.

Once you learn to recognize, track, and share signs, I think you'll be amazed at how often your loved ones, Spirit Guides, angels, and the Divine are speaking to you every day.

Chapter 15

Rule #5: Do Your 100%

The fifth and final rule of receiving is "Do your 100%." Interestingly, this was one of the first rules I started to understand and ingest, long before I developed The Receiving Method™ as a system and these rules as its foundation.

I consider it the final "rule," but if you embrace only this one, I promise things are going to get a lot easier!

Most of us grow up believing that if something—ANYTHING—is going to happen in our lives, we have to make it happen. But believing that it's all on our shoulders is what keeps us from allowing the Divine to step in and help us—or allowing in any help from anyone.

But even after we start to understand that there is a loving Universal Force who wants to support us and make this whole life easier, we usually end up wondering, "What part am I supposed to play in making it all happen?"

Even if we accept that manifestation exists and that there are gifts flowing to us, don't we need to do *something* to make it all come together?

If we want a better job, we know we can't just sit around, waiting for it to just show up—we have to do *something*, right?

So how do we know how much is our part to do and where the Divine takes over?

That is where the 100% rule comes in.

When we do our 100% (no matter how big or small), then the Universe steps in and does the heavy lifting on our dreams. Our 100% is the amount of effort we can reasonably put in without moving us into a place of depletion.

Since most of us exist in a constant state of depletion and exhaustion, doing your 100% might primarily involve resting to bring your energy reserves back to the "full" level. Society exists at a collective exhaustion level because we are rarely taught how to surrender, how to let go of making it all happen.

In fact, we are taught just the opposite message. In most places on Earth at this point in our human evolution, we are dominated by a dysfunctional productivity bias. There is a belief that when we are doing something we are more productive (and therefore more valuable) then when we are still or "being." Although we might learn the value of stillness, our unconscious programming still whispers we are better when we are working than when we stop.

This programming makes it hard for us to tap into the inner wisdom that knows when it is time to slow down or even stop. This constant busyness and resulting depletion short-circuits our inner guidance system, the part of us that understands when it's time to stop, surrender, and move into a place of faith.

So how do we reconnect to this inner wisdom and begin to understand when we've done "enough"?

Well, I can tell you that it likely starts with a big, long rest. When I'm working with large groups of people and ask them what their soul most wants and needs right now, 60 percent of the audience will immediately answer "a nap." As the discussion continues, another 20 to 30 percent of the room will eventually concede that their true answer is either a nap, a day off, or a vacation. What is even crazier is that when I ask people why they didn't give that answer initially, they say it's because it didn't feel like a "real" answer. They didn't even know they were allowed to ask for that! They believed that any instinct for rest was "fake." That's how productivity-addicted we all are.

Most people in those same audiences will tell me they feel lost, exhausted, or depleted and want to feel alive again. They want to have fun and feel like they have purpose in the world. They will also tell me that they really, really want to learn their language—to understand how to communicate more clearly with their own intuition, their Spirit Guides, and their loved ones.

If I asked them if they knew how to get out of "depletion" and get back that sense of playfulness and magic, they would have said "no." Those same people would say they have no idea where to begin in connecting to their intuitive gifts—yet they all have the answer. They had it the minute I asked, "What does your soul most need and want right now?" Rest. The answer is for them to STOP DOING.

In order for us to have a full, exciting, connected life, we need to learn to stop at our 100% and surrender the remaining efforts to the Divine.

So how do we know what our 100% is? When you start tuning into what is yours to do and what is meant to be surrendered to the Divine, it can be challenging to tell. As I said, we have a dysfunctional productivity bias, so it's almost too much for us to comprehend that bringing a goal to life can happen without doing everything ourselves. If we aren't making it happen, how will it get done? This is why learning to create space for magic is critical. It shows us the how; it shows us "the magic."

The most exciting part of learning this 100% rule is that you can create bigger goals, embrace bigger dreams. Most of us limit ourselves to creating what we reasonably know we can bring to life. We do this because of our productivity bias (the belief that it's all on our shoulders). If it's completely up to us to bring a goal to life, of course those goals are going to be smaller than if we believe we can create them in partnership with the limitless Divine.

And if you are one of the unique creatures who already embraces dreams much bigger than yourself, harnessing the 100% rule is going to help you go after them without exhausting yourself.

Wendi Finds the Promised Land

This is what happened for Wendi. As I shared earlier, she left a corporate job and launched her own business. She is one of those "make it happen" kind of people, so once she set a goal to create $250,000 of revenue, she also put together a plan that would have had her working ALL THE TIME.

But part of her reason for heading out on her own was to create more time and freedom to be available for her teen daughter, so we worked together to apply the 100% rule and give her more space in her week. Furthermore, we built in a couple of weeks' vacation. At first, Wendi balked. She was launching a new business—how could she take a vacation?

But I explained to her that she hadn't had proper rest in some time. Vacation was part of her 100%. I also showed her that her original plan was based on the belief that only she was doing the heavy lifting. When she reduced the amount of work she planned to do, she wasn't setting herself up to fail; she was giving the Universe the permission to help. She kept her goal the same size but shared the effort in creating with the Divine.

We mapped out a new, more reasonable outreach plan that gave her space to breathe, rest, and enjoy her life. Furthermore, she was still grieving the loss of her dad. I told her she needed to make space for crying and missing him. This would allow her to grieve naturally, and the Divine wanted to support her in doing that.

At first Wendi was scared. She wondered if this new plan was "responsible." She had grown up believing the "responsible" thing was to work as hard as possible to make her dreams a reality, and she wondered if she was putting her family at risk by "letting go."

I assured her over and over that it was more responsible to pull in help from the limitless Divine than try to do it all on her own.

After a few weeks passed, she told me, surprised, "Oh my goodness, Patty. I can't believe it! It's working. We already have a few requests for proposals! I never would have believed that would happen with this level of effort!"

Within three months, Wendi had signed her $250,000 in clients. The best part was that she had done it in a way that truly honored her goals. She had spent time at the beach connecting to her dad. She had taken her teen daughter on vacation. She had eaten dinner with her family. She didn't have to sacrifice her joy, peace, or happiness for financial stability.

This is what happens when we do our 100% and let the Divine step in to take us to the finish line.

Of course, you might be thinking, if the Divine can do so much, why do we have to do anything? The answer is that we chose to incarnate in this human form so that we could experience our creative powers in this limited human form. We want to be part of the process, and there are important soul-expanding lessons we learn in doing our 100%.

For Wendi, she loves making deals. She enjoys building partnerships, so all this initial work is fun for her. Part of her soul expansion in this life is to learn to trust and enjoy balance. For me, helping others learn to embrace the 100% rule is about experiencing the exhilaration of being human.

Here's the thing about doing our 100%. Holding onto our big dreams but not doing all the work to get there—in other words, truly surrendering—takes us right to the edge of our own vulnerability. Instead of creating a false sense of security by always doing, doing, doing, we allow ourselves to experience our own inner divinity—the ability to create and experience something beyond our limited human capabilities.

Doing our 100% is like being on a trapeze bar and having the courage to release our grasp of the bar so we can experience both flight and getting to a new place (the next trapeze bar). In order to experience that flight—to taste the sweetness of those moments, suspended mid-air with nothing holding us there but the momentum of our dreams—we have to believe the Divine has already sent us that next bar to grasp. We have to let go of what we know to grasp what's possible.

Even if you're ready to take flight, you're still probably wondering, "How do I know where my 100% is?"

The answer is simple but not always easy to tap into. Your 100% is anything that feels like inspired action. Inspired action is something that either feels exciting to do or energizes you to complete. In Wendi's case, making six calls a week energized her, but her original plan had her making fifteen calls a week, which felt heavy. Six calls were her "energy edge," and so that was her 100%.

How can you tell when you've passed your "100%"? If it feels like you're pushing a boulder up a hill, you've gone past your 100%.

You may be sitting there and saying, "Well, that's great, Patty, but EVERYTHING feels like I'm pushing a boulder up a hill. Does that mean I do nothing?" And the answer is . . . yep, pretty much.

You may not be able to effectively stop doing *everything*, but if life feels like pushing a boulder up a hill, it means you are in deep need of rest. In fact, your 100% right now is to schedule rest—lots of it.

For many women that feels very scary. Even the idea of resting sparks the thought, "If I take time off, who will _____?" (feed the kids, take care of my parents, make enough money, etc.).

I get it. It is scary to rest. Everything you've learned in your life has told you that rest is bad, lazy, proof that you aren't doing "enough." I promise you nothing is further from the truth. For every person I've worked with, when they finally summoned the courage to really disconnect from their lives for a week or two (or at bare minimum, power way down), magic has arrived in the most surprising ways.

Wendi's biggest client signed just after she got back from vacation. But what was an even bigger win was that she finally felt the connection she so deeply desired with her daughter.

Rest and Receive

Another client, Erin, a high-end make-up artist, was looking for a brick-and-mortar space to take her business to the next level but couldn't find anything in her price range. She took two weeks off, completely disconnected from her business, and a landlord spontaneously reached out to offer her a ridiculously low-priced space upon her return.

Lou, my most cynical receiver ever, took a week off from his business (for the first time ever in his entire career) and upon return had his best year ever—which he says can only be attributed to his time off.

Susie, who spent all day every day helping her special needs child navigate the world and getting the help he needed, was contemplating divorce because she felt resentful of her husband's ability to leave every day and his perceived unwillingness to support their child in the same way she did. Upon leaving for a week (which scared her so much she almost canceled ten times between the time she booked a trip with her girlfriends and finally left), she returned to find her husband doing more with their son than he had done since their son was born.

I have endless stories of the magic that happens on the other side of rest. If you are exhausted, numb, frustrated, or feel alone, I promise you the first step to finding the balance of your 100% is to take some time away from all your activity.

Rest is the key to creating space for magic.

The Universe wants to help you. And what is so fun about this is that many times the Universe will send other humans to help too. So you won't just feel supported and loved by a Divine Being you can't touch or see—you'll start to see all the humans who are ready, willing, and able to create some of that magic for you.

A couple of months after my dad died, I was headed to a Girl Scout Encampment weekend. I was one of the leaders but was arriving late because of a previous commitment. It had been a really tough week for a lot of reasons.

Before I got there, one of the leaders had suggested they wait until I arrived to assign the girls their encampment duties (things like cleaning the bathrooms). This was something I typically did, because if someone needed to be the "tough mom," it was usually me. My friend Steph jumped in and told the other leaders that I had enough on my plate, and she was sure some-one else could handle this. When she told me she had done this, I cried. I cried hard.

In the grand scheme of my life, assigning bathroom duties to the Girl Scouts was pretty low on the effort scale, but I can tell you, in that moment something broke open in me. That was the first time in my life that someone had lifted a burden off me before I understood it was there and would be too much for me. It felt like I had been breathing exhaust fumes and suddenly breathed my first fresh breath in a long time.

That is what happens when we learn to slow down and honor our 100%. The Divine and other humans will reveal to us on the most profound level that we are seen, that we are not alone, and that we are loved.

Conclusion

I think back now on that woman I was back when Katie was a baby. That woman sitting there in that rocking chair, holding her precious little girl, and feeling completely lost and disconnected from herself, her life, and all its blessings.

I can honestly say I have become the mother she deserves. The problem was never that I wasn't giving my baby girl enough. The problem was that I wasn't giving *me* enough. Back then and to this day, I'd walk through fire for each of my kids. That hasn't changed.

What has changed is that I've walked through fire for myself. I've walked through the fire of my fear that if I let go, no one will be there to catch me. I've learned that the Divine is always there, and that has created all the space for magic I have today.

During the height of isolation of the COVID pandemic, my daughter was just on the cusp of her teen years. It's such a vulnerable time, and to have the pressure cooker of a pandemic define that transition was hard. I listened as she told me heartbreaking stories of how her friends were struggling with depression, self-harming, and anxiety.

"How are you doing, Katie girl, in all this?"

She said, "I feel guilty because I'm so okay. I wish we could be together, but I'm good. Really, really good. Mom, I know I'm this okay because I have the mom I have."

That moment is anchored in my heart. It isn't that I'm a better mom—that's not what she was saying. What she was saying was that I showed her what it looked like to trust that it's going to be okay. You can't tell another person that—all you can do is embody it and hope they feel it. My daughter did.

I'm often asked how you help someone else make space for magic. The answer is—you can't. But if you do your work and walk through your fires, then you can show them what it looks like, and that is the only control we have.

By the way, did you catch the part where my daughter said she felt guilty that she was so okay? Yeah, so did I. Obviously we both have some work to do with being okay with being so good.

Creating space for magic isn't a destiny—it's a journey. And I'm so grateful I have my kids to show me where my next step is. Wherever you are on your journey of creating space for magic, I want you to know I'm here with you on the path. Perhaps I'm a few steps ahead—or maybe you're a few steps ahead of me.

Either way, I'm glad we are on this journey together. It is my firm belief that each of us who incarnated on this planet at the same time did so knowing the other would be here. We may never meet on Earth, but I know in my heart that before we came, we agreed to come together.

The world is a better place because you are here. Thank you for having the courage to come. Being human can be hard, but if you make space for magic, it will be easier.

Acknowledgments

The one thing that has sustained me through every experience in my life is my faith in the Divine. That faith was the greatest gift my parents gave me. It was my experience with each of them, both on this side of the veil and the next, that taught me to see and find magic. Mom and Dad, I love and miss you and feel you in every page here. Thank you.

To The Receiving School® community and especially those that allowed me to share their stories here I am both humbled and honored that you let me play a role in your life path. We are all walking this journey together.

Azul, you are the first person who pulled the words "Space for Magic" from the ethers of my heart and gave definition to the idea of this book that lived inside me. You believed in it and saw it for what it could be. Bless you.

Clara, Ursula, Shari, and Ricki, there is a special place in heaven for first readers. Thank you for wading through the miasma of early writing and telling me what was good and how to make it better. Your insight and attention gave me courage to put this out into the world.

Katie and Matthew, my loves, you show me every day what matters and has meaning. You are my teachers and being your mom is a privilege. Thank you for caring about this book and about me through the writing. You are each wise beyond your years.

Matt, thank you for believing in me, even when I wobble in that faith. You have always been the quiet voice of confidence in who I am and who I can become. You didn't blink when the corporate banker you married took another path, and that is a testament to your heart. I love you.

About the Author

PATTY LENNON is a best-selling author, keynote speaker, certified coach, and founder of The Receiving School®.

She is a former type-A corporate banker who discovered there was more to living than making money. She left banking to help others do the same.

She is a certified coach with a master's in psychology and has been featured in *Forbes*, *Fast Company*, and *Daily Worth*. She blends brain science and metaphysics to help her fellow humans find clarity, focus, and inspiration so they can easily manifest their dreams into reality.

Patty hasn't found a crystal shop or bookstore she can't get lost in, though she loathes shopping in all other forms. She loves chocolate, autumn in New England, and watching her two teens discover what lights them up.

Patty can be found on the web at www.pattylennon.com and on Facebook at www.facebook.com/pattyalennon.

I would appreciate your feedback on what chapters helped you most and what you would like to see in future books.

If you enjoyed this book and found it helpful, please leave a REVIEW on Amazon.

Visit me at

WWW.PATTYLENNON.COM

WWW.FACEBOOK.COM/PATTYALENNON

Thank you!

CPSIA information can be obtained
at www.ICGtesting.com
Printed in the USA
LVHW051044241021
701359LV00007B/155